Manual 1

YOUNG WOMEN
Fun-tastic! Activities

You'll find activities to match Lessons #1-49:

❀ Young Woman's Value-able Journal
❀ Lesson Activities to Place in Journal
❀ Midweek Activities
❀ Thought Treats
❀ Scripture Cards

D1616586

❀ *"Bloom Where You're Planted"*
7 Floral Symbols to Color-Code Value Journal

GOSPEL BASIC SUBJECTS:

Attitude   Covenants   Dating   Drug Abuse   Education   Example

Forever Families   Family Support   Forgiveness   Friendship   Goals

Happiness   Health Care   Heavenly Father   Holy Ghost   Homemaking

Honoring Parents   Jesus Christ   Leadership   Media Influences

Prayer and Meditation   Potential   Priesthood   Purity   Records

Repentance   Righteousness   Sabbath Day   Scriptures

Second Coming   Self-care   Self-improvement   Self-reliance

Service   Success   Talents   Temptation   Testimony   Time

Virtue   Virtue and Truth   Word of Wisdom   Work

Covenant Communications, Inc.
American Fork, Utah

Printed in the United States of America
First Printing: September 1999

Young Women FUN-TASTIC! Activities - Manual 1
ISBN 1-57734-514-2

ACKNOWLEDGMENTS: Thanks to Inspire Graphics, Inc., for the use of Lettering Delights computer fonts.

Meet the Creators of *Young Women Fun-tastic! Activities* and Many Popular Creative Teaching Tools

PRIMARY PARTNERS: Lesson Activities and more
Nursery and Age 3 (Sunbeams) Vol. 1	+ CD-ROM
Nursery and Age 3 (Sunbeams) Vol. 2	+ CD-ROM
CTR A and CTR B Ages 4-7	+ CD-ROM
Book of Mormon Ages 8-11	+ CD-ROM
Old Testament Ages 8-11	
New Testament Ages 8-11	+ CD-ROM
Doctrine and Covenants Ages 8-11	
Achievement Days, Girls Ages 8-11	
Sharing Time: Faith in Jesus Christ	+ CD-ROM
Sharing Time: Baptismal Covenants	+ CD-ROM

Primary Partners: Clip-Art on CD-ROM (500 images)	
Primary Partners Singing Fun!	+ CD-ROM

FAMILY HOME EVENING:
File Folder Family Home Evenings	+ CD-ROM
Home-spun Fun Family Home Evenings 1	+ CD-ROM
Home-spun Fun Family Home Evenings 2	+ CD-ROM

YOUNG WOMEN:
Young Women Fun-tastic! Activities Manual 3
Young Women Fun-tastic! Activities Man. 1 + CD-ROM
My Fun-tastic! Personal Progress Planner and Journal
for *Beehive 1* and *Beehive 2* (detailed below)

MARY H. ROSS, Author

Mary Ross (shown left) is an energetic mother, and has been a Primary teacher and Achievement Days leader. She loves to help children and young women have a good time while they learn. She has studied acting, modeling, and voice. Her varied interests include writing, creating activities and children's parties, and cooking. Mary and her husband, Paul, live with their daughter, Jennifer, in Sandy, Utah.

JENNETTE GUYMON-KING, Illustrator

Jennette Guymon-King (shown right) has studied graphic arts and illustration at Utah Valley State College and the University of Utah. She served a mission to Japan. Jennette enjoys sports, reading, cooking, art, gardening, and freelance illustrating. Jennette and her husband, Clayton, live in Riverton, Utah. They are the proud parents of their daughter Kayla Mae and son Levi.

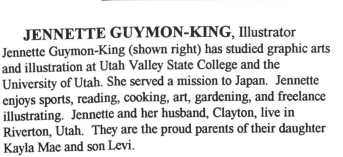

INTRODUCING
My Fun-tastic!
PERSONAL PROGRESS
Planner and Journal
Beehive 1 and Beehive 2

Achieving Personal Progress goals can be easy if each young woman has her own planner and journal. Each planner/journal contains all the goals found in the *Personal Progress* book with matching fun borders. All of the goals are planned for the young woman, making it easy for her to fill in the details as she achieves each goal. Then, in the journal portion she can record her goal experiences. This makes it easy for the Young Woman leader to track her progress.

My Young Women
Value-able Journal

photo

I will bloom
where I'm planted.

"Thou shalt be like a watered garden."
Isaiah 58:2-14

INTRODUCTION
Fun-tastic! Young Women Activities:
*Lesson Lifesavers and More for Manual 1**

Young Women leaders, you'll find the following activities
to match lessons #1-49 to help young women
"Bloom Where They Are Planted."

❀ Lesson Activities   ❀ Midweek Activities
❀ Thought Treats   ❀ Scripture Cards
❀ Young Woman's Journal with
7 Value Divider Tabs to Store Activities
❀ 7 Floral Symbols to Identify Values

❀ Many of the midweek activities in this book were contributed by Fern
Law, a Young Women leader of six years. Her comments about the book:
*"The activities in this book focus on Jesus Christ and his gospel. They will
encourage young woman to search within themselves and feel deeply the
love and devotion of their Savior, and to be a light unto the world."*

How to Use This Book:

❀ <u>**Lessons #1-49 Table of Contents**</u> helps you locate lesson
activities quickly.

❀ <u>**A-Z Table of Contents**</u> helps you locate activities by subject.

❀ <u>**Lesson Activities**</u> coordinate with
specific parts of the lesson (for
example, Lesson #8 Family Life Can
Be a Picnic tent card complements
page 30 in the Young Women Manual, as shown right).

Review Story (page 30) in
Young Women Manual. 1*.

Life with my family can be a picnic if I
understand my role as a wife and mother.
Wife: Mother:

❀ <u>**Midweek Activities**</u> add to and enhance your lessons with a
lesson follow-up activity during the next
week. This keeps the subject open for
discussion, giving more meaning to the lesson
taught on Sunday. IDEA: Use the first 10-15
minutes of your midweek activity to present a
lesson match midweek activity. Many of the
midweek activity ideas can take up the entire
evening.

❀ <u>**Scripture Cards**</u> (pages 108-
124) encourage young women to
learn a value-able scripture each
week. Fill in the blanks and color
the floral symbol.

My Testimony Grows as I Study the Scriptures

HAPPINESS: I Will Find Joy in Everyday Living

Alma 41:10 "Do not suppose, because it has
been spoken concerning restoration, that ye
shall be _ _ _ _ _ _ _ _ from _ _ _ _
to happiness. Behold, I say unto you, wickedness
never was happiness."

John 13:17 "If ye know these things, happy are ye if ye
_ _ _ them."

Young Women Value: Choice & Accountability (orange poppy) Lesson #6 Manual 1

*Young Women Manual 1 and Personal Progress books are published by The Church of Jesus Christ of Latter-day Saints, Salt Lake City, Utah.

INTRODUCTION (page 2)

❀ **Personal Progress* Goals** are cross referenced with each week's lesson. To motivate goal achievement, spotlight young women who have achieved these specific goals, having them share their experiences.

❀ **ORGANIZE JOURNAL AND ACTIVITIES.**
1. Set Up Journals. Help young women set up their journal. Select a three-ring binder for each young woman. Copy the seven value cover pages and value tabs (on the pages that follow).

2. Identify Floral Symbols. The floral symbols (shown above) found on the activities and scripture cards will help young women identify the values: Faith (white lily), Choice & Accountability (orange poppy), Good Works (yellow sunflower), Integrity (purple pansy), Knowledge (green ivy), Divine Nature (blue morning glory), and Individual Worth (red rose).

3. Color-Code Journal by coloring the floral symbol hidden on most of the activities (sample shown right). Paper punch activity page, and place activity in journal binder behind the value tab. Encourage young women to post the activity to review during the week before placing activity in their journal. POCKETS: Place pockets on the back of journal pages by cutting paper in thirds and gluing 1/4-inch on bottom and sides. Place odd sized activities in pockets.

❀ **Thought Treats** teach lesson concepts (when appropriate). Many treats can be delivered during the week or used during midweek activities to reinforce gospel learning. Attach motivational notes to treats, e.g., Lesson #9 "Mom and Pop Lollipops." NOTE IDEA:

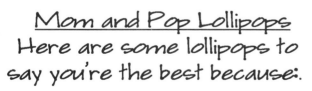

❀ **Evening of Excellence** is a great time for young women to display their Young Woman's Value-able Journal. Each week they can collect activities and handouts to store in their journal. Parents will delight in their daughters' grasp of gospel subjects. Girls can also display their scrapbooks and Personal Progress journals.

*Young Women Manual 1 and Personal Progress books are published by The Church of Jesus Christ of Latter-day Saints, Salt Lake City, Utah.

TABLE OF CONTENTS
Young Women FUN-TASTIC! ACTIVITIES - Manual 1

Introduction: LESSON and MID-WEEK ACTIVITIES to Make Learning Fun!

A-Z Preview of Lesson Activities #1-49

Young Woman's Value-able Journal (dividers and tabs)

My Testimony Grows as I Read the Scriptures (scripture cards for Lessons #1-49) 108-124

*Young Women Manual 1 is published by The Church of Jesus Christ of Latter-day Saints, Salt Lake City, Utah.

TABLE OF CONTENTS

Young Women FUN-TASTIC! ACTIVITIES - Manual 1

Lessons #22-49	ACTIVITIES	Pages:

Young Women Manual 1 is published by The Church of Jesus Christ of Latter-day Saints, Salt Lake City, Utah.

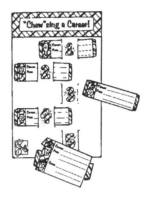

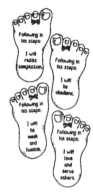

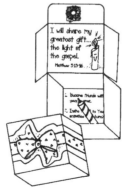

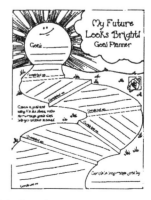

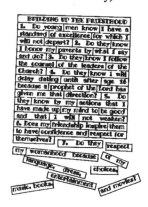

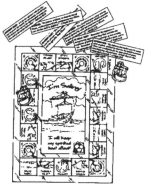

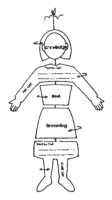

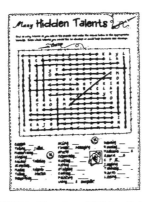

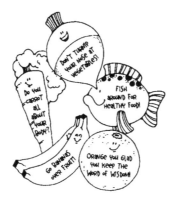

Divider Tabs for Young Women Value-able Journal

HOW TO PLACE TABS ON DIVIDER SHEETS:

1. Copy tabs on white cardstock paper.
2. Color floral symbols: Faith (white), Divine Nature (blue), Individual Worth (red), Knowledge (green), Choice & Accountability (orange), Good Works (yellow), and Integrity (purple).
3. Cover with clear contact paper to reinforce tabs.
4. Cut out and fold above word line, i.e. fold above "Faith."
5. Glue or tape tab on divider page in order of the seven values.
6. You will also find tabs for Calendar, Family Home Evening, Friends, Personal Progress, and Notes

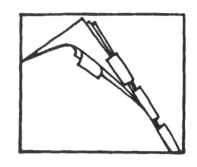

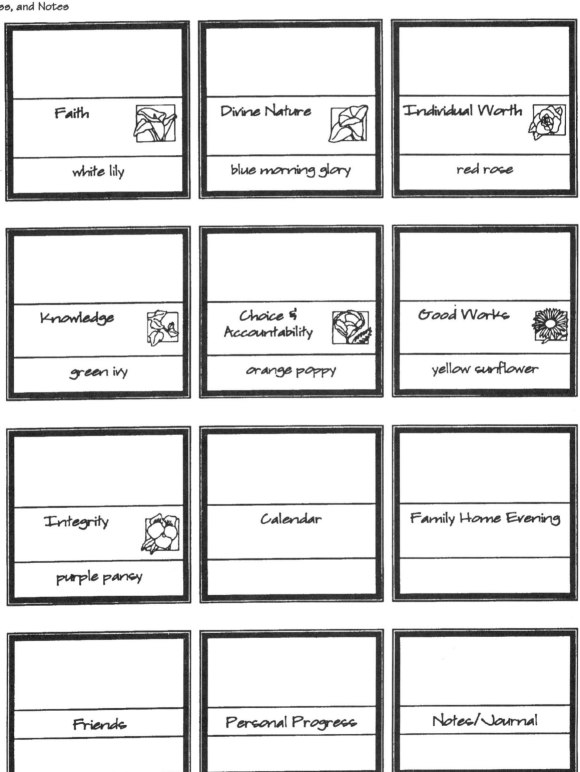

Faith	Divine Nature	Individual Worth
white lily	blue morning glory	red rose
Knowledge	Choice & Accountability	Good Works
green ivy	orange poppy	yellow sunflower
Integrity	Calendar	Family Home Evening
purple pansy		
Friends	Personal Progress	Notes/Journal

My Young Women
Value-able Journal

photo

I will bloom
where I'm planted.

"Thou shalt be like a watered garden."
Isaiah 58:2-14

I Am of Great Worth and Value ...
According to My Heavenly Father Who
Knows Me Perfectly

Value: Faith

(white lily)

"I am a daughter of Heavenly Father
who loves me, and I will have faith in
his eternal plan, which centers in
Jesus Christ, my Savior."

"And, if you keep my commandments and
endure to the end you shall have eternal life, which
gift is the greatest of all the gifts of God."
D&C 14:17

I Am of Great Worth and Value ...
According to My Heavenly Father Who
Knows Me Perfectly

Value: Divine Nature

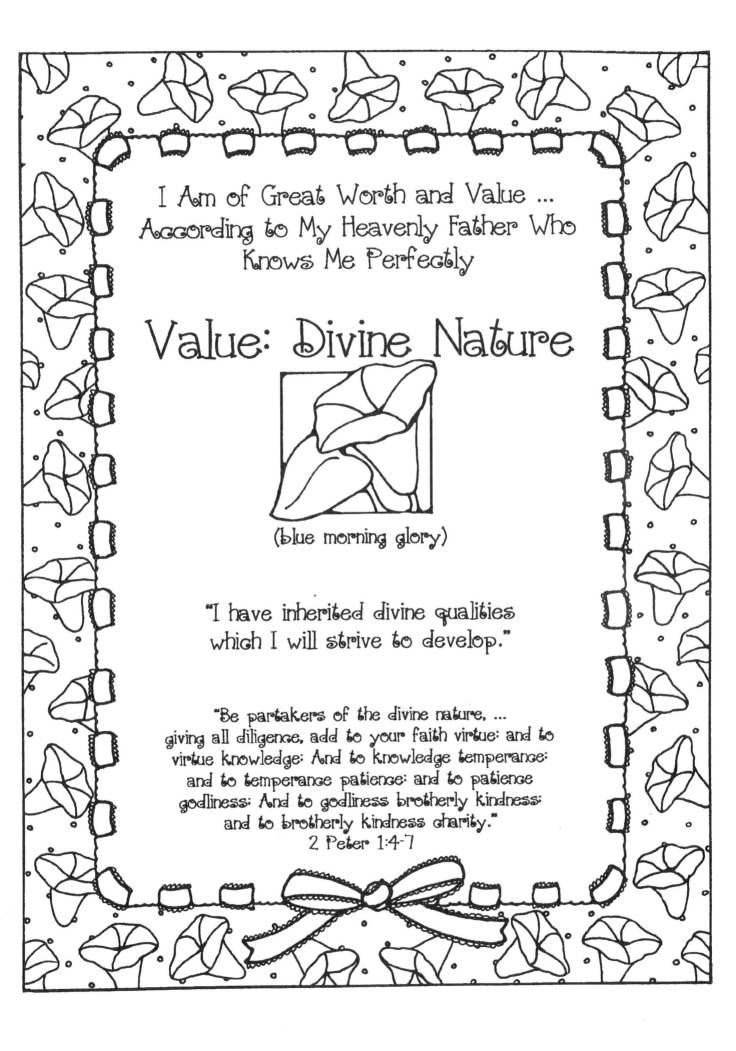

(blue morning glory)

"I have inherited divine qualities
which I will strive to develop."

"Be partakers of the divine nature, ...
giving all diligence, add to your faith virtue: and to
virtue knowledge: And to knowledge temperance:
and to temperance patience: and to patience
godliness: And to godliness brotherly kindness:
and to brotherly kindness charity."
2 Peter 1:4-7

I Am of Great Worth and Value ...
According to My Heavenly Father Who
Knows Me Perfectly

Value: Individual Worth

(red rose)

"I am of infinite worth with my
own divine mission which I
will strive to fulfill."

"Remember the worth of souls is
great in the sight of God."
D&C 18:10

I Am of Great Worth and Value ...
According to My Heavenly Father Who
Knows Me Perfectly

Value: Knowledge

(green ivy)

"I will continually seek
opportunities for learning
and growth."

"Seek learning, even by study
and also by faith."
D&C 88:118

I Am of Great Worth and Value ...
According to My Heavenly Father Who
Knows Me Perfectly

Value: Choice & Accountability

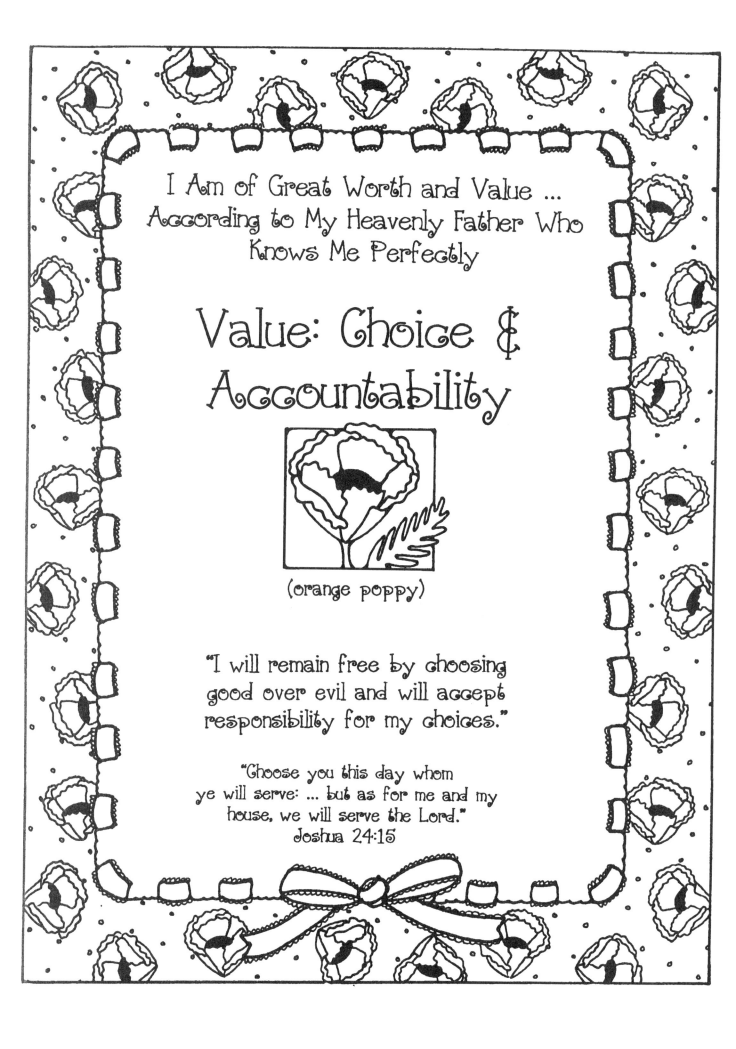

(orange poppy)

"I will remain free by choosing
good over evil and will accept
responsibility for my choices."

"Choose you this day whom
ye will serve: ... but as for me and my
house, we will serve the Lord."
Joshua 24:15

I Am of Great Worth and Value ...
According to My Heavenly Father Who
Knows Me Perfectly

Value: Good Works

(yellow sunflower)

"I will nurture others and build the
kingdom through righteous service."

"Therefore let your light so shine
before this people, that they may see your good
works and glorify your Father who is in heaven."
3 Nephi 12:16

I Am of Great Worth and Value ...
According to My Heavenly Father Who
Knows Me Perfectly

Value: Integrity

(purple pansy)

"I will have the moral courage to
make my actions consistent
with my knowledge of right
and wrong."

"Till I die I will not remove
mine integrity from me."
Job 27:5

Lesson #1	**HEAVENLY FATHER:** I Am a Daughter of God *(Drawing Nearer to My Heavenly Father goal poster)*

YOU'LL NEED: Copy of goal poster (page 2) for each young woman, pencils, and markers.

Review Discussion (page 4) in Young Women Manual 1*.

ACTIVITY: Help young women suggest ways they can improve their relationship with their Heavenly Father.
1. Color poster.
2. Study the following scriptures to learn that we show our love to Heavenly Father by keeping his commandments and by serving others. Scriptures: D&C 88:63, Mosiah 2:17, John 14:15, and Matthew 25:40.
3. Write on the poster how you will draw closer to Heavenly Father. See the box (and Thought Treat) for ideas found in the lesson discussion.

COLOR SYMBOL: Color floral symbol on activity and scripture card. File activity in Young Women Value-able Journal behind value tab.

Divine Nature (blue morning glory)

PERSONAL PROGRESS* GOALS:
Beehive 1 (Individual Worth 8)
Beehive 2 (Faith 7, Divine Nature 8, Integrity 4)
Mia Maid 1 (Faith 4, 7, 9, Integrity 7)
Mia Maid 2 (Integrity 5)

THOUGHT TREAT: One Eternal Round Mints. Share Starlite or Star Brite mints, where the pink pinwheel design goes round and round, never ending. Give the following note with mints.

Heavenly Father has always been there for us and he will always be there for us. His plan proves that he has always "mint" for us to be happy. All we need to do to be happy is to pray and listen after we pray, keep his command-"mints," show our gratitude, study his word in the scriptures, and listen to his prophets.

MIDWEEK ACTIVITIES:
1. **Sacred Yearly Letter.** Talk about patriarchal blessings and about earthly fathers—what they want for their children and what they do for their children. Discuss what Heavenly Father does and wants for his children, and things he gives us to help us. Have young women write a letter of appreciation to their Heavenly Father and put it in a sealed envelope. Tell them to nourish these feelings so they will grow. Have them put the letter in their journal for one year. They can then write another letter to Heavenly Father, expressing appreciation and love, then read the letter from the last year. Repeat this every year. Each year they can see their love grow as they read their thoughts and see them increase in love.
2. **Send a Letter Home.** Give each young woman a helium balloon and ask her to take the balloon home. When she is alone, she can write a note to Heavenly Father on the balloon with a marker, sharing her gratitude for what he has done and listing her personal goals. After she signs it, she can let it go soaring toward heaven.

Drawing Nearer to My Heavenly Father

I will do the following to draw closer to my Heavenly Father:

○ _____

○ _____

○ _____

○ _____

○ _____

○ _____

D&C 88:63
Mosiah 2:17
John 14:15
Matthew 25:40

Lesson #2	**JESUS CHRIST: I Will Think of My Savior** *(Gifts of Resurrection and Eternal Life stand-up gift)*

YOU'LL NEED: Copy of gift (page 4) for each young woman, scissors, 8-inch ribbon, pencils, paper punch, and markers.

> *Review Scripture Discussion (Alma 11:42-43, and 11:40; page 7) in Young Women Manual 1*.*

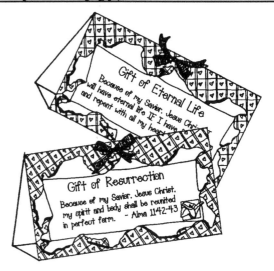

ACTIVITY: Help young women create a stand-up gift that identifies two important results of Jesus Christ's atonement. Alma 11:42-43 (the gift of resurrection) and Alma 11:40 (the gift of eternal life).
1. Color and cut out card on outside edge leaving the center piece (bottom of card).
2. Fold the bottom of card.
3. Pull together top pieces of card back to back and paper punch two holes at the top where indicated.
4. Thread a ribbon through holes and tie a bow.
5. Option: Enclose treat below inside gift.

COLOR SYMBOL: Color floral symbol on activity and scripture card. File activity in Young Women Value-able Journal behind value tab.

> *Faith (white lily)*

PERSONAL PROGRESS* GOALS:
<u>Beehive 1</u> (Faith 2, 4)
<u>Beehive 2</u> (Faith 2, Integrity 4)
<u>Mia Maid 1</u> (Faith 7, 9, Divine Nature 2, 4, 6)
<u>Mia Maid 2</u> (Divine Nature 3, 4, Integrity 2, 5)

THOUGHT TREAT: <u>Hourglass Rice Krispies Cereal Treat</u>. TO MAKE: Melt 3 tablespoons margarine and marshmallows in a large bowl. Marshmallow choices: 1 (10 oz.) package, 40 regular sized marshmallows or 4 cups of miniature marshmallows. Add 6 cups Kellogg's Rice Krispie cereal and stir. Lightly butter a 12x9x2-inch pan and place treats in pan. Cut treats into 6" x 2" bars and wrap in clear plastic wrap. Tie two different strings tightly in a bow

in the center of the treat to create an hourglass shape. Option: Enclose treat inside gift.
OBJECTIVE: Tell young women that the hourglass represents our time here on earth, and this hourglass-shaped treat reminds us of the sweet blessings Heavenly Father has given us. He has given us a special gift with no strings attached (cut off one string). This gift is the gift of resurrection. The second gift of eternal life has a string attached (leave second string on). We must earn this special gift if we want to spend all eternity with our families and with our Heavenly Father and Jesus who love us. Remember our potential is great and we can receive this gift if we use our time wisely.

MIDWEEK ACTIVITIES:
<u>Turn Our Faces Toward the "Son."</u>
To encourage young women to feel the warmth that can come from having Jesus Christ in their lives and to see things clearly with his light, begin by setting up a room with a sun lamp. Talk about repentance and the Atonement. Turn out the lights and talk about Satan's plan. Tell how some people see physically (the light), but they do not see spiritually (the light of Christ). Blindfold the young women, and talk about how some see spiritually, but do not see physically. We can see with our heart.

Gift of Resurrection

Because of my Savior, Jesus Christ, my spirit and body shall be reunited in perfect form.   ~ see Alma 11:42-43

Gift of Eternal Life

Because of my Savior, Jesus Christ, I will have eternal life IF I have faith in him and repent with all my heart. ~ see Alma 11:40

Lesson #3	**EXAMPLE: I Will Follow the Example of Jesus Christ**
	(In His Footsteps mirror motivators)

YOU'LL NEED: Copy of mirror motivators (page 6) on colored cardstock paper for each young woman, scissors, and markers.

Review Chalkboard activity (page 9) in Young Women Manual 1*.

ACTIVITY: These mirror motivators will remind young women to walk in the footsteps of Jesus.
1. Color and cut out feet.
2. Post on mirror during the week (one each week).
3. Practice the quality or trait posted on the foot for five days, checking the box and/or painting a toe nail each day with real polish or markers.

COLOR SYMBOL: Color floral symbol on activity and scripture card. File activity in Young Women Value-able Journal behind value tab.

Divine Nature (blue morning glory)

PERSONAL PROGRESS* GOALS:
Beehive 1 (Faith 4, Divine Nature 7, Knowledge 3, Integrity 1, 2)
Beehive 2 (Divine Nature 8, Choice & Accountability 2, 6, 8, Integrity 4, 5, 7, 8)
Mia Maid 1 (Faith 7, Divine Nature 2, 6, Choice & Accountability 7, Integrity 7)
Mia Maid 2 (Divine Nature 3, 4, Individual Worth 3, Choice & Accountability 3, Integrity 2, 3)

THOUGHT TREAT: Footstep Fudge. Make footprints out of white or chocolate fudge. Place miniature M&M's or small candies on toes. To make footprints, melt white or sweet chocolate chips in microwave, adding 1 can sweetened condensed milk and 1 teaspoon vanilla. Mold into feet and lay on waxed paper.

MIDWEEK ACTIVITIES:
1. Tie a Yellow Ribbon Example Night. Have young women take the challenge of Sister Ames (Story, page 11) from the lesson* to "Live for twenty-four hours as if Christ were right beside you, seeing everything you do." Tie a yellow ribbon around their finger or wrist, and ask them to wear the

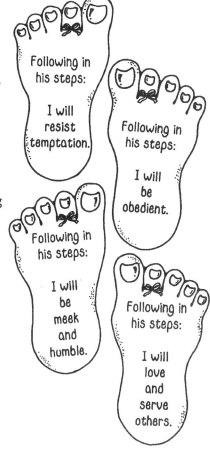

Following in his steps:
I will resist temptation.

Following in his steps:
I will be obedient.

Following in his steps:
I will be meek and humble.

Following in his steps:
I will love and serve others.

ribbon when they are home to remind them to act as if the Savior were there. Tell them that the tradition of tying a yellow ribbon around a tree is a symbol that you look forward to someone's coming home (the yellow ribbon is a symbol of acceptance and love). (Option: Sing the song "Tie a Yellow Ribbon ['Round the Old Oak Tree]" written by Irwin Levine, music by L. Russel Brown. Challenge young women during the week to think about and look forward to the Savior's coming by living as he did, by following his example. During the Yellow Ribbon Example Night, tie a bunch of yellow ribbons to decorate the chairs or tables or pictures as you talk about the Savior. Have young women share their experiences during the week. Follow up in the next few weeks so young women can develop the habit of living as the Savior would live. During your discussions, ask, "Was it hard at first?" "Did it get easier?"
2. What If? Night. Use Marion G. Romney's example of solving dilemmas through searching the scriptures and praying. Have a large jar with "What if's" written (e.g., challenging questions but also easy ones, e.g., "What if you get a scholarship to Harvard and BYU?" Or, "What if a nonmember asks you to a party?" Some can be sensitive questions but still real to today's youth. Be tactful as you search for the Lord's way. Acknowledge that some questions and answers take a lot of searching the scriptures, pondering, and praying.

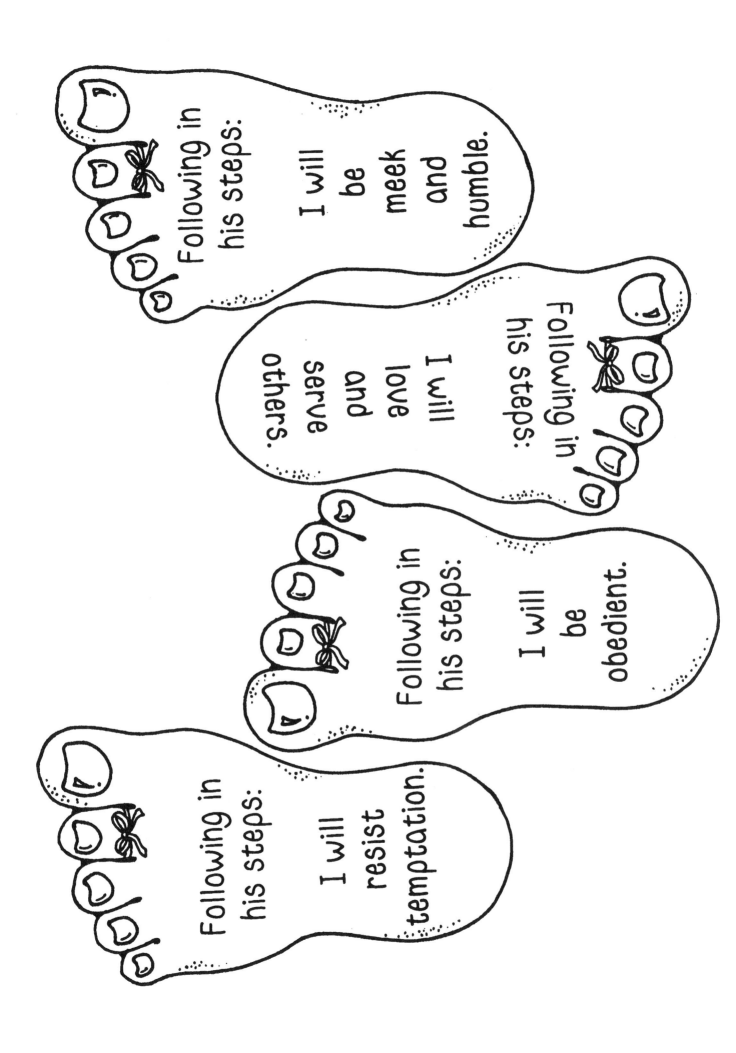

Following in his steps:

I will be meek and humble.

Following in his steps:

I will love and serve others.

Following in his steps:

I will be obedient.

Following in his steps:

I will resist temptation.

Lesson #4 — HOLY GHOST: I Will Seek the Companionship of the Holy Ghost
(Light of the Holy Ghost mobile)

YOU'LL NEED: Copy of light bulbs (page 8) on cardstock paper, a 12-inch ribbon for each young woman, scissors, pencils, and markers.

> *Review Chalkboard discussions (pages 13-14) in Young Women Manual 1*.*

ACTIVITY: Color and cut out light bulbs and glue back to back. Paper punch at the top. Tie a 12-inch ribbon at the top so young women can hang mobile in their room. Look up scriptures for clues to the missing words. <u>Light bulb #1 (Worthiness)</u>: what we must do to be worthy of the companionship of the Holy Ghost. ANSWERS: (1) repent, (2) pray, (3) faith, (4) world, (5) baptized. <u>Light bulb #2 (Blessings)</u>: different ways that the Holy Ghost can bless our lives. ANSWERS: (1) teach, (2) things, (3) truth, (4) record, (5) comforter, (6) mind, heart.

COLOR SYMBOL: Color floral symbol on activity and scripture card. File activity in Young Women Value-able Journal behind value tab.

> *Divine Nature (blue morning glory)*

PERSONAL PROGRESS* GOALS:
<u>Beehive 1</u> (Divine Nature 5)
<u>Beehive 2</u> (Divine Nature 3, 4, Choice & Accountability 1)
<u>Mia Maid 2</u> (Divine Nature 2, 5, Integrity 5)

THOUGHT TREAT: <u>Clutter Cookies</u>. For each young woman, frost a sugar cookie and top with "clutter" (dried fruit, chocolate chips, candies, broken lifesavers). Next, frost a sugar cookie for each young woman and decorate it with a simple frosting flower. As young women eat, remind them to keep their lives free from clutter and other things that are not of value. This way we can make room for the Spirit of the Holy Ghost to enter our mind and heart to guide us, to help us find happiness, and to make eternal life decisions.

MIDWEEK ACTIVITY:
<u>Stop and Smell the Flowers—Compare to the Spirit of the Holy Ghost.</u> Follow Steps #1-7:

<u>Step #1.</u> Create a room full of clutter with a bouquet of flowers in the center of the table. Have dirty dishes on the table. Scatter magazines, papers, and clothes all over the floor. Have a dust cloth, vacuum, and a pan of dish soap and a dish cloth to wash dishes available. Ask young women to enter the room, sit down, and write down their feelings.

<u>Step #2.</u> Ask young women to go out, but have a few stay and help clean up the room. Leave the bouquet of flowers in the center of the table.

<u>Step #3.</u> Ask young women to come back into the room and write down their impressions.
Say, "The bouquet of flowers you see can be compared to the Holy Ghost in our lives. The first time you saw this room, you saw a room full of clutter. You may not have noticed the flowers. But when the room was free of clutter, you might have seen the flowers first. This is how it is with the Holy Ghost. When our minds are free of clutter, we are free to listen to and enjoy Heavenly Father's spirit."

<u>Step #4.</u> Make a list of things that clutter our lives that might prevent us from listening to the Spirit (for example, not doing homework, not going to church, not reading the scriptures, not helping around the house, not going to seminary, etc.)

<u>Step #5.</u> Blindfold one of the young women, saying, "Sometimes we blindfold ourselves with things that don't matter and neglect the things that do matter."

<u>Step #6.</u> Give each young woman a small bouquet of flowers with a note that reads:

With the Holy Ghost, I can bloom where I am planted.

<u>Step #7.</u> Talk about the floral symbols assigned to each value (e.g., rose represents Individual Worth). Have them ask themselves what their life would be like without one of these values. Each value invites the Spirit of the Holy Ghost.

Blessings of the Holy Ghost

○

1. _____ you all things.
2. Shows us _____ to come.
3. Manifests the _____ of all things.
4. Bears _____ of the Father and the Son.
5. Is the _____ .
6. Reveals things to your _____ and _____ .

1. John 14:26   2. John 16:13   3. Moroni 10:4-5   4. D&C 42:17   5. D&C 39:6   6. D&C 8:2

Be Worthy to Receive the Holy Ghost

○

1. _____ of my sins.
2. Obey Heavenly Father's _____ .
3. _____ for the companionship of the Holy Ghost.
4. Ask in _____ .
5. Forsake the _____ and live.
6. Be _____ and true to my covenants.

1. Mosiah 4:10   2. Deut. 11:27   3. 3 Nephi 19:21   4. 1 Nephi 15:11   5. D&C 53:2   6. 3 Nephi 26:17

Lesson #5	**POTENTIAL: I Will Develop My Divine Potential** *(Finding Joy Monthly Time Capsule)*

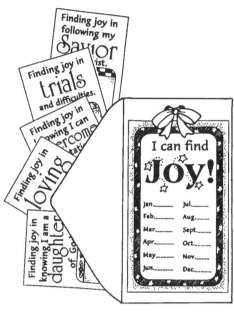

YOU'LL NEED: Copy of time capsule cards and envelope label (page 10), a small envelope and an 8-inch ribbon for each young woman, scissors, glue, paper punch, and markers.

> *Review Teacher discussion and testimony (page 18) and Reading (page 19) in Young Women Manual 1.*

ACTIVITY: (1) Color and cut out five time capsule cards and envelope label. (2) Glue label on an envelope. (3) Have young women write their goals or thoughts on each card. (4) Enclose cards in envelope. (5) Paper punch two holes at the top of envelope; tie a ribbon/bow. (6) Ask young women to review the time capsule cards each month to remind them to seek their divine potential. (7) Have them place a check (√) by each month as they open and read the contents of the time capsule envelope.

COLOR SYMBOL: Color floral symbol on activity/scripture card. File activity in Young Women Value-able Journal behind the value tab.

> *Divine Nature (blue morning glory)*

PERSONAL PROGRESS GOALS:
Beehive 1 (Divine Nature 1, Choice & Accountability 4, 5, Integrity 3)
Beehive 2 (Divine Nature 1, Individual Worth 8, Choice & Accountability 1, 7)
Mia Maid 2 (Divine Nature 6, Individual Worth 2)

THOUGHT TREAT: Follow Jesus Footstep Fudge. Mix and melt togther two 7-ounce bags of chocolate or butterscotch chips, 1 can sweetened condensed milk and 1 teaspoon vanilla. Mold into feet shaped and place on waxed paper. Use miniature M&Ms to create toes. Tell girls they can develop their divine potential as they follow in the footsteps of Jesus.

MIDWEEK ACTIVITIES:
1. Joyful Things to Do. Read 2 Nephi 28:30 (*"line upon line precept upon precept"*). Talk about how exciting life is, always learning new things! Have young women choose a skill or something they want to do to develop their potential. Conduct a workshop to develop these skills (e.g., sewing, cooking, nursing, balancing a checkbook, preparing for a career).

2. Valuable Mirror Reflections.
Step #1: Have young women go into a room where they can look into a large mirror or you can give each one a hand mirror. Ask them to really look at themselves and to smile.
Step #2: Ask them to take another look in the mirror this next week and talk to themselves about their potential. Ask them to smile and tell themselves that they are daughters of Heavenly Father and that they are of great worth and value. Tell them that if they do this day after day then one day they will come to believe that they are truly daughters of God and that they are deeply loved. This realization will help them have true joy.

3. Friends with Heavenly Father.
Ask young women to talk to Heavenly Father as they would their best friend. Heavenly Father wants us to go to him as we would a close friend and trust in his guidance. Have young women write down on paper things they would like to pray to Heavenly Father about. Ask them to choose something to pray about this week and listen to the Spirit. Tell them that the Spirit will guide them with warm positive feelings when they are on the right path. Friends can help them, but Heavenly Father is their best friend, and he is their true source of knowledge and joy.

I can find

Joy!

Jan._____	Jul._____
Feb._____	Aug._____
Mar._____	Sept._____
Apr._____	Oct._____
May_____	Nov._____
Jun._____	Dec._____

Finding joy in trials and difficulties.

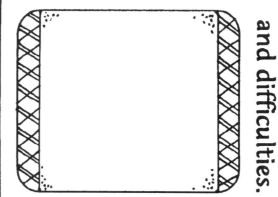

Finding joy in knowing I can overcome temptation.

Finding joy in following my Savior Jesus Christ.

Finding joy in knowing I am a daughter of God.

Finding joy in

loving
myself.

Lesson #6	**HAPPINESS:** I Will Find Joy in Everyday Living
	(happiness mirror motivators and goal list)

YOU'LL NEED: Copy of mirror motivator and goal list (page 12) on colored paper for each young woman, scissors, pencils, and markers.

Review Lesson Application (page 23) in Young Women Manual 1*.

ACTIVITY: #1 Happiness Mirror Motivator: Help young women memorize the Harold B. Lee quote and post on their mirror as a reminder that happiness comes from within. Talk about the outward trials and how we can gain strength and joy by focusing on the gospel of Jesus Christ, through prayer and scripture study, keeping the commandments, and serving others.

#2 Goal List Mirror Motivator: Write ways they can find joy now to remind them to work on in coming weeks, e.g., "Find a need and fill it."

COLOR SYMBOL: Color floral symbol on activity and scripture card. File activity in Young Women Value-able Journal behind value tab.

Choice & Accountability (orange poppy)

PERSONAL PROGRESS* GOALS:
Beehive 1 (Divine Nature 1, Knowledge 2, Integrity 1)
Beehive 2 (Individual Worth 1, 3, 4, 8, Choice & Accountability 8)
Mia Maid 1 (Divine Nature 7, Individual Worth 1, 5, Choice & Accountability 1, 5)
Mia Maid 2 (Choice & Accountability 5)

THOUGHT TREAT: Hidden Smile and Frown Sandwich Cookies. Pull open 16 sandwich cookies (e.g., Oreos or vanilla cream cookies.) With a butter knife, carve a smile or frown inside the frosting of each cookie (8 smiles and 8 frowns). Place top back on cookies. Have young women open cookies and name a happy choice when they open up a smile cookie or choice that brings unhappiness if they open up a frown cookie.

MIDWEEK ACTIVITIES:
1. Rose-colored Day. Tell young women that having joy in their day is all in the way they look at it. You can look at your day with rose colored glasses or dark glasses. Looking on the bright side requires 15-second thought changes when things don't look bright. For example, when studying for a test, talking to someone you don't know well, or cleaning your room or the bathroom, take the first 5 seconds to decide that you want a better attitude, the next 5 seconds to decide on the attitude, and the next 5 seconds to repeat that positive attitude.
JOY-LESS THOUGHTS: "I hate this." "I'd rather be watching TV." "They don't like me."
JOY-FUL THOUGHTS: "This will bring my mom happiness." "It will feel good to have this clean." "Someday I will use this in college or to teach my future child." "I will invite her to go."
2. Shape Up Your Day Brainstorm. Give girls a slip of paper and have them (either alone or with another girl) come up with different ways to look at their day and challenging situations. Tell them that they can shape their day any way they want to if they look on the bright side. Then their day will be in great shape.
THOUGHT TREAT: Joy Jigglers. Have a pan of Jello ready with knives to cut and eat shapes.

"Happiness does not depend on what happens outside of you but what happens inside of you."

—Harold B. Lee

What I can do to find joy now. . .

Lesson #7	**HOMEMAKING:** I Will Find Joy in Homemaking *(Heavenly Homemaker Coupon Book for mom or dad)*

YOU'LL NEED: Copy of coupons and coupon book cover (pages 14-15) on colored paper (cardstock paper for each young woman, scissors, stapler, and markers.

> *Review Teacher presentation "when the family expresses gratitude" (page 25) in Young Women Manual 1*.*

ACTIVITY: Encourage young women to express their thanks to their mother or father by helping at home. Give parents this coupon book and encourage them to use their daughters' homemaking service. (1) Color and cut out coupon book. (2) Place Heavenly Homemaker on the top and place two staples at the left to hold book together.

COLOR SYMBOL: Color floral symbols on activity and scripture card. File activity in Young Women Value-able Journal behind value tab.

Good Works (yellow sunflower)

PERSONAL PROGRESS* GOALS:
Beehive 1 (Divine Nature 1, Good Works 2, 4, 5)
Beehive 2 (Knowledge 1, Integrity 3)
Mia Maid 1 (Knowledge 1-4)
Mia Maid 2 (Knowledge 1)

THOUGHT TREAT: Sweet Home Gingerbread Cookies. Cut out large gingerbread house cookies. Paint windows and a door using a paint brush and colored milk (1/4 teaspoon food coloring to 2 tablespoons canned milk). Bake until golden brown. Tell young women that home can be a sweet place to be if it is taken care of.

MIDWEEK ACTIVITIES:
1. **Home-spun Demo.** Have individuals who iron, cook, vacuum, dust, sew, or wash windows well demonstrate their skills in rotating classes.

They might iron a shirt, make a simple soup, boil eggs, tell how to clean with a toothbrush, use Clorox without bleaching clothes in the process, take stains out of laundry, sew a zipper or collar, make button holes, sew on a button, etc. Give prizes for participants, e.g., a duster, a sponge, a can of ironing spray starch, a wire whisk.

2. **Homemaking Talent Night.** Have moms and young women display and tell about their talents, e.g., an ironed shirt, a cooked or baked item, a picture of a decorated room, a window washing demonstration, a sewn item, a gardening demo. Invite moms and have fun sharing talents. Share homemade bread and jam.

3. **Home Sweet Home Ideas.** Have young women bring several ideas that have made their home a pleasant place to live. Have them tell when they feel most comfortable at home, how they feel when the house is in order and clean, what they do when a guest is coming, how they feel when the guest arrives. Talk about home neglect (sweeping the dirt under the rug), piling junk in cupboards, closets, and drawers, leaving things out, clutter, and dirty dishes. Talk about strategies to keep the home in order and what they do to share their support and love. BEFORE YOU START, prepare a bag with dirty laundry, smelly socks, and sweaty gym clothes. Have young women close their eyes while they smell the contents. Then have them close their eyes and smell a bag of clean clothes (dried on the clothesline or with air freshener sprayed inside). Talk about the odors that come from a dirty house and the clean smell that comes from a clean house. Share "home sweet home" ideas.

Good for one free
_____
_____

Good for one free
_____
_____

Heavenly Homemaker

Coupon Book

To: _____
From: _____

Lesson #8   **ATTITUDE: I Want to Be the Best Possible Wife and Mother**
(Family Life Can Be a Picnic tent card)

YOU'LL NEED: Copy of tent card (page 17) for each young woman, scissors, pencils, and markers.

> *Review Story (page 30) in Young Women Manual 1*.*

ACTIVITY:
1. Help young women realize that attitude is the key to a happy home. Life can be a "picnic" (or at least, a lot easier) if we have the right attitude.
2. Write on this tent card those roles of a wife and mother that help make family life more enjoyable.
3. Color and cut out tent card, cutting along the family top lines with a razor blade or Exacto knife.
4. Encourage young women to create a positive environment while they are living at home. Then when they are living with roommates or have a home of their own, they will be in the habit of creating a positive environment, where friendship and love can endure.

COLOR SYMBOL: Color floral symbol on activity and scripture card. File activity in Young Women Value-able Journal behind value tab.

> *Individual Worth (red rose)*

PERSONAL PROGRESS* GOALS:
Beehive 1 (Divine Nature 1, 2, 6, Knowledge 1, Good Works 5, Integrity 1)
Beehive 2 (Individual Worth 3, 4, 8, Choice & Accountability 8, Good Works 4)
Mia Maid 1 (Divine Nature 1, 4, 5, 7, 8, Choice & Accountability 5)
Mia Maid 2 (Individual Worth 4, Good Works 1)

THOUGHT TREAT: Picnic. Spread a blanket on the floor and provide a sack lunch (with sandwich, chips, banana, and a drink) for each young woman. On the sack write:

Life with my family can be a picnic if I understand my role as a wife and mother.
Wife: Mother:

My life can be a picnic if each day I "sandwich" in some scriptures reading, "chip" in and help others, go "banana"s with service, and "drink" freely from the fountain of knowledge.

MIDWEEK ACTIVITIES:
1. International Night. Have several women of different nationalities come and talk about their roles as wives and mothers. Have visitors express their feelings about their callings as wives and mothers, and the influence the world has. Discuss the similarities in their roles as they strive to do what their Heavenly Father wants them to do. Have refreshments from the different nationalities (include recipes).
2. A Man's Opinion Panel. Have a panel of husbands and young men. Ask them to share their thoughts about their wives or mothers and what makes the "best" mom or a "great" wife. Prepare questions ahead of time to ask panel.

Life with my family can be a picnic if I understand my role as a wife and mother.

Wife: Mother:

Lesson #9	**HONORING PARENTS: I Will Improve My Relationship**
	(Super Dad and Mom Spotlight)

YOU'LL NEED: Copy of Super Dad and Super Mom Spotlight (pages 19-20) for each young woman, pencils, and markers.

Review Suggested Activities #1-4 (page 36) in Young Women Manual 1*.

ACTIVITY: Encourage young women to honor their parents using this Super Dad and Mom Spotlight form.

OPTION #1. Use form to spotlight parents and give positive highlights from their lives (or from their lives since the birth of the young woman). These could be read during an "Honor Parents" night.

OPTION #2. Use form to write a plan with brothers and sisters how they will express honor and appreciation to parents. Then carry out the plan.

OPTION #3. Use forms to write a letter of appreciation to parents.

OPTION #4. Use form to write personal goals to show honor and respect to parents. Then work on those goals.

COLOR SYMBOL: Color floral symbol on activity and scripture card. File activity in Young Women Value-able Journal behind value tab.

Individual Worth (red rose)

PERSONAL PROGRESS* GOALS:
Beehive 1 (Divine Nature 4, 6, 7, 8, Individual Worth 5, Good Works 6)
Beehive 2 (Divine Nature 8, Individual Worth 5, Integrity 3)
Mia Maid 1 (Divine Nature 1, Individual Worth 3, 4)
Mia Maid 2 (Divine Nature 7, Individual Worth 5)

THOUGHT TREAT: Mom and Pop Lollipops. Give each young woman three lollipops with two tied together with a ribbon to give to their parents, with the following note attached and completed:

Mom and Pop Lollipops
Here are some lollipops to say you're the best because:

MIDWEEK ACTIVITY: Parent Appreciation Night.

Step #1. The week before, have young women write a note to their parent(s) or guardian with at least four points of appreciation. Leaders could secretly tie each note (with parents' name on top) to a pretty plastic fork with a pretty ribbon. Leaders could also write a note to each young woman, expressing specific points of appreciation and attaching a fork (with name on note).

Step #2. Young women invite their parents, grandparents, or guardian to a dinner.

Step #3. Serve a spaghetti and salad dinner without eating utensils. Provide handy wipes to wipe hands before and after the meal.

Step #4. After the meal, a leader says,

"Just like this fork [hold fork up], we often take many things for granted that our young women and parents do for us. Tonight we would like to honor our young women and parents, and express our points of appreciation (point to points on fork). Each young woman has prepared a note expressing their points of appreciation, and we the leaders have a note expressing our points of appreciation to our young women. Thank you. We will now serve dessert and you will be able to eat with your forks."

Step #5. Pass out individualized forks with notes attached to each individual.

Step #6. Serve dessert with a different fork.

Step #7. Optional Favors: Place a flower on moms' plates and a Big Hunk candy bar on dads' plates.

*Young Women Manual 1 and Personal Progress books are published by The Church of Jesus Christ of Latter-day Saints, Salt Lake City, Utah.

Super Mom

Spotlight!

Lesson #10	**FAMILY SUPPORT: I Will Support and Be Loyal to My Family** *(Lend a Hand Spin-and-Support wheel)*

YOU'LL NEED: Copy of wheel and spinner (page 22) and a metal brad for each young woman, scissors, and markers.

Review Lesson Application (page 41) in Young Women Manual 1*.

ACTIVITY: Encourage young women to lend support to specific members of their family each day by creating and spinning this support wheel.
1. Color and cut out wheel and spinner.
2. Attach spinner to wheel with a metal brad at the wrist. Punch and tie a string to hang spinner after use.
3. Each day of the week girls can spin the wheel and concentrate on giving support to that person.
4. When landing on Secret Choice, they choose a family member to show support and love to anonymously.
5. When landing on Someone in Need, they choose a family member to watch to become aware of that person's needs so they can help.
6. Encourage young women to use this for a family home evening lesson on family support. Family members can secretly spin the wheel and give anonymous support to the person they spin or choose.

COLOR SYMBOL: Color floral symbol on activity and scripture card. File activity in Young Women Value-able Journal behind value tab.

Individual Worth (red rose)

PERSONAL PROGRESS* GOALS:
Beehive 1 (Divine Nature 3, 7, 8, Knowledge 1, Good Works 3, 5, 6, 8)
Beehive 2 (Faith 2, Divine Nature 5, 6, 7, 8, Individual Worth 5, Good Works 1, 2, 5, 6, Integrity 3)
Mia Maid 1 (Faith 6, Divine Nature 3, 5, 7, Individual Worth 6)
Mia Maid 2 (Divine Nature 1, 8)
Laurel 1 & 2 Project #1 (page 79)

THOUGHT TREAT: Cookie Clock. Decorate a round sugar cookie by frosting and adding candies

and frosting clock hands. Tell young women that if they plan their time well they can make time to support and enjoy their family, creating lasting memories and family ties.

MIDWEEK ACTIVITIES:
Self-image Building Workshop. Tell young women that we are self-image builders. Before the workshop, have someone who is a builder prepare some precut boards; have nails, hammers, scotch tape, and glue available. Have young women in groups build a project without nails. Give them scotch tape, string, and glue. Demonstrate how the finished project is shaky and may not stand up under pressure. Bring out nails and hammer, and proceed to redo it using nails. Project is now much more sturdy. Discuss our ability to supply nails in building up others or our building our self-image. If we supply only a tape, glue, or string type of support, the support doesn't last. Discuss situations that build confidence. Create a favor by nailing two boards together and then nailing this note to the board:

When times get tough and you need to be strong, you can draw on your inner strength. Build yourself and your family to withstand life's challenges.

2. Family Support Cookie House. Construct a graham cracker house with frosting and decorate with candies. Have young women take it to their families and say, "I made this house for you to show you that I love and support you."

Lesson #11	**SELF-RELIANCE: I Will Follow My Savior** *(D&C 29:1-2 Ways to Follow Savior tent card)*

YOU'LL NEED: Copy of tent card (page 24) for each young woman, pencils, and markers.

Review Scripture discussion (page 45) in Young Women Manual 1*.

ACTIVITY: Help young women memorize D&C 29:1-2 and talk about the maturity that comes from listening and following the Savior.
1. Color, cut out, and fold tent card to stand up.
2. Write ways they will follow the Savior Jesus Christ. (Ideas: be humble, pray, listen to the Lord, obey the commandments, serve others, read the scriptures, attend church.)

COLOR SYMBOL: Color floral symbol on activity and scripture card. File activity in Young Women Value-able Journal behind value tab.

Divine Nature (blue morning glory)

PERSONAL PROGRESS* GOALS:
Beehive 1 (Divine Nature 7)
Beehive 2 (Divine Nature 8, Integrity 2, 7)
Mia Maid 1 (Divine Nature 2, Individual Worth 5, Choice & Accountability 1)

THOUGHT TREAT: Breaded Baby Chick Eggs. Shape bread dough into egg shapes. Dip in melted butter and drop into a bag of colored sugar and shake. To make colored sugar, mix 1/4 cup sugar and 2 or more drops of food coloring in a bag. Bake 15-20 minutes at 350. Place eggs in a basket or bowl. Tell young women that baby chicks must break through the shells without help; if the shell is forced open, the baby chick will die. We too need to push past our obstacles to develop self-reliance and maturity. As we listen to and rely on the Savior for help, we gain the maturity and strength to overcome our trials in life.

MIDWEEK ACTIVITIES:
I Think I Can Classes. Set up several classes for the young women: one on budget by a CPA, one on job interviews by a person who hires, one on grooming by a beautician, one on organizing time by an organized individual, etc. Have a 15-minute class just to cover the basics. If there is a large group, you could break off into workshops and have the individual teach four times. If instructors are willing, write their names and phone numbers on a card for each girl with a logo that shows their specialty, e.g., $ (budget), a resume page (job interviews), a mirror (beautician), or a clock (organizing time).

TAKE HOME FOOD FAVOR: Pass out cans of juice or fruit with the label taken off and replaced with a label that reads:

Enjoy this treat and think about the things you "can" do as you learn correct principles and apply them.

Ways I will follow the Savior:

"Listen to the voice of Jesus Christ, your Redeemer, the Great I AM, whose arm of mercy hath atoned for your sins; Who will gather his people even as a hen gathereth her chickens under her wings, even as many as will hearken to my voice and humble themselves before me, and call upon me in mighty prayer."

D&C 29:1-2

Lesson #12	**SELF-RELIANCE: I Will Strengthen My Family Relationships** *(Good Apple Attitudes poster)*

YOU'LL NEED: Copy of Good Apple Attitudes Family Goals poster (page 26) for each young woman, pencils, and markers.

> *Review Preparation #4 (page 47) in Young Women Manual 1*.*

ACTIVITY:
1. Color and read poster.
2. Talk about attitudes or actions that can spoil family relationships, and attitudes that can strengthen them.
3. Encourage young women to take this poster home and set goals with their family that will strengthen their family relationships. On each apple, write a family member's name and how you will strengthen your relationship with that person.

COLOR SYMBOL: Color floral symbol on activity and scripture card. File activity in Young Women Value-able Journal behind value tab.

> *Individual Worth (red rose)*

PERSONAL PROGRESS* GOALS:
Beehive 1 (Divine Nature 7, 8, Knowledge 1, Good Works 3, 5, 6, Integrity 1)
Beehive 2 (Divine Nature 5, 6, 7, 8, Individual Worth 1, 5, Good Works 1, 2, 4, 6, Integrity 3)
Mia Maid 1 (Faith 6, Divine Nature 3, 5, 7, Individual Worth 6, Choice & Accountability 1)
Mia Maid 2 (Divine Nature 1, 8, Individual Worth 4)
Laurel 1 & 2 Projects #1, 21 (page 79)

THOUGHT TREAT: Dehydrated or Fresh Apples. As you eat the apples, talk about the seeds found in each one. One seed can create an apple tree, just as one thought or attitude can create a positive or negative atmosphere in the home. We can plant the seeds of kindness, happiness, patience, love, and respect each day.

MIDWEEK ACTIVITY: Home Sweet Home. Help young women make a gingerbread or a graham cracker house for someone in their family, or their whole family, to show their support. Attach a note telling ways they will support that family member or the whole family. Idea: Copy the following note for young women, and draw or glue real nails on the side by each set of kind uplifting words.

If one bad apple attitude can spoil the family bushel, what can I do to help family life taste sweet?

TO: _____

FROM: _____

I built this house for you to show you that I support you in the following ways:

_____

_____

_____

_____

_____

_____

Good Apple Attitudes

If one bad apple attitude can spoil the family bushel, what can I do to help family life taste sweet?

Lesson #13

PRIESTHOOD: I Will Honor Priesthood Bearers
(Building Up the Priesthood building blocks puzzle)

YOU'LL NEED: Copy of building blocks puzzle (page 28), a letter size envelope, and a blank 8 ½-inch x 11-inch sheet of paper for each young woman, scissors, glue, and markers.

ACTIVITY: Help young women think about their ability to positively influence priesthood bearers with this building blocks puzzle.

> *Review Quotation by Sister Ardeth Kapp #1-7 (pages 54-55) in Young Women Manual 1*.*

1. Cut out building blocks ahead of time for young women and place in an envelope.
2. Read the quote aloud. Ask young women to listen carefully, because you will give them a quiz afterwards.
3. Give them the puzzle pieces in the envelope, glue, and an 8 ½-inch x 11-inch piece of paper.
4. QUIZ: Ask them to place the puzzle pieces on the blank sheet of paper from #1-7, showing ways they can build up and strengthen bearers of the priesthood.
5. Glue puzzle pieces into place.

COLOR SYMBOL: Color floral symbol on activity and scripture card. File activity in Young Women Value-able Journal behind value tab.

Individual Worth (red rose)

PERSONAL PROGRESS* GOALS:
Beehive 1 (Knowledge 8)
Mia Maid 1 (Faith 1, Good Works 1)

THOUGHT TREAT: Brick Wall Cookies.
1. Stack 4-5 graham crackers or wafer cookies on top of each other, using frosting in between.
2. Tell young women we can build up the priesthood holders as we live the gospel standards and help them to live these standards also. If we do this, they will be ready when it's time for them to serve missions. As we build them up, they in turn can build others up. Brick by brick, we can build ourselves up and also the young men we influence. The wall of positive influence continues to grow and grow. This shows how just one simple thing we do can affect so many people.

MIDWEEK ACTIVITIES: Sustaining Priesthood Bearers.
This activity can also be used for the Lesson #16 Midweek Activity. The objective is to help young women uphold, defend, and support deacons, teachers, and priests in their callings.

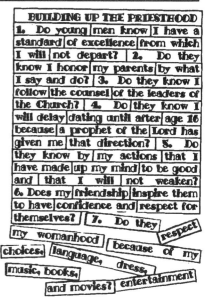

BUILDING UP THE PRIESTHOOD
1. Do young men know I have a standard of excellence from which I will not depart? 2. Do they know I honor my parents by what I say and do? 3. Do they know I follow the counsel of the leaders of the Church? 4. Do they know I will delay dating until after age 16 because a prophet of the Lord has given me that direction? 5. Do they know by my actions that I have made up my mind to be good and that I will not weaken? 6. Does my friendship inspire them to have confidence and respect for themselves? 7. Do they respect my womanhood because of my choices, language, dress, music, books, and movies? entertainment

1. Plan and prepare a surprise breakfast for the young men. The young men can be told by their leaders that they are needed at the church (with no reason given). Leaders will need to bring the young men to the designated place for the breakfast. (You could also invite their leaders and perhaps the bishopric. They can alert parents that it will not take long.) Have a big fun breakfast with hash browns, pancakes, eggs, juice, and muffins the young women have prepared.
2. Prepare thank-you notes ahead of time, placing them under the young men's plates. Express thanks for the support and leadership of the priesthood, and encourage the young men to continue to honor it and live by its principles.
3. Then have a fun game of coed volleyball, broom hockey, or "Wink-um." (detailed below). The young men leaders can then take them home.

HOW TO PLAY WINK-UM:
1. Have young men sit on chairs (in a circle) with one chair vacant.
2. Young women stand behind chairs.
3. The young woman behind the vacant chair winks at a young man who races to the vacant chair.
4. The girls try to keep the young men from escaping by holding their shoulders (but girls have to keep their arms straight down).
5. Switch places after 15 minutes.

BUILDING UP THE PRIESTHOOD

1. Do young men know I have a standard of excellence from which I will not depart? 2. Do they know I honor my parents by what I say and do? 3. Do they know I follow the counsel of the leaders of the Church? 4. Do they know I will delay dating until after age 16 because a prophet of the Lord has given me that direction? 5. Do they know by my actions that I have made up my mind to be good and that I will not weaken? 6. Does my friendship inspire them to have confidence and respect for themselves? 7. Do they respect my womanhood because of my language, dress, entertainment choices, music, books, and movies?

Lesson #14	**PRIESTHOOD: I Will Support My Father in Righteousness**
	(Lily Pad of Reminders word scramble)

YOU'LL NEED: Copy of Lily Pad word scramble (page 30) for each young woman, pencils, and markers.

Review Chalkboard discussion and Lesson Application (pages 58-59) in Young Women Manual 1*.

ACTIVITY: Give each young woman a Lily Pad Reminders list to "Hop on in and figure out how to support our dads!" Have young women unscramble the words on each lily pad and write them in the space provided. Encourage young women to try one each week to improve their relationship with their father.

ANSWERS: (Left column): <u>Build</u> him up, say <u>kind</u> and <u>thoughtful</u> things. Be <u>cheerful</u> and <u>helpful</u> at home. Support him in <u>family home evening</u>. (Center column): Ask for a <u>father's blessing</u>. Seek his <u>advice</u> and <u>counsel</u>. Give him <u>love</u> and <u>appreciation</u>. (Right column): Share <u>concerns</u> and interests. Get to <u>know</u> him. Be <u>obedient</u>. Spend <u>time</u> together. Set a good <u>example</u> to <u>brothers</u> and <u>sisters</u>.

COLOR SYMBOL: Color floral symbol on activity and scripture card. File activity in Young Women Value-able Journal behind value tab.

Individual Worth (red rose)

PERSONAL PROGRESS* GOALS:
<u>Beehive 1</u> (Individual Worth 3, Integrity 3)
<u>Mia Maid 1</u> (Good Works 1)

THOUGHT TREAT: <u>Lily Pad Pudding</u>. Make some pistachio Jello pudding and plop some on small but sturdy paper plates. As young women eat their pudding, have each one share a positive experience they have had with their father.

MIDWEEK ACTIVITIES:
1. Dandy Dads Night. Plan an evening of fun and games with dads. Games: balloon toss,

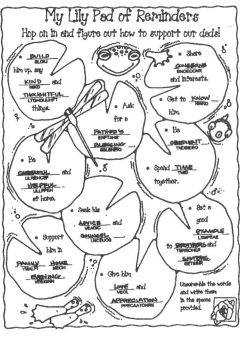

gunny sack, 3-legged or relay races, frisbee baseball, Nerf baseball. Serve barbequed burgers and the fixin's with a picnic on blankets on the lawn or the floor in the recreation hall. Allow time for young women to express their love for and gratitude to their fathers. Those who do not have their dads there can bring a grandfather, special uncle, brother, or guardian.

2. Project with Dad. Do a science project, yard work, painting, or hammer and nail project with Dad.

3. Homemade Card. Make Dad feel like the star in your life by making a homemade card. IDEAS: ☆Have young women bring candy bars to make a candy bar card on poster paper for their dad. ☆Bring art supplies, nails, magazine pictures, stamps, buttons, golf Ts, etc., to glue on card. ☆Create pop-up cards. ☆Create a letter card, writing a letter to slip inside a specially designed cover or envelope. ☆Create a book card by writing a history of your experiences with your dad in a book entitled, "A Book About Me and My Dad." ☆Draw pictures of you and your dad and tell about them. ☆Make a thumbprint card using a stamp pad and your thumbprint to create Dad's favorite animals or animals you have had in your family. Young women could also write about their experiences with their dads and family pets.

My Lily Pad of Reminders
Hop on in and figure out how to support our dads!

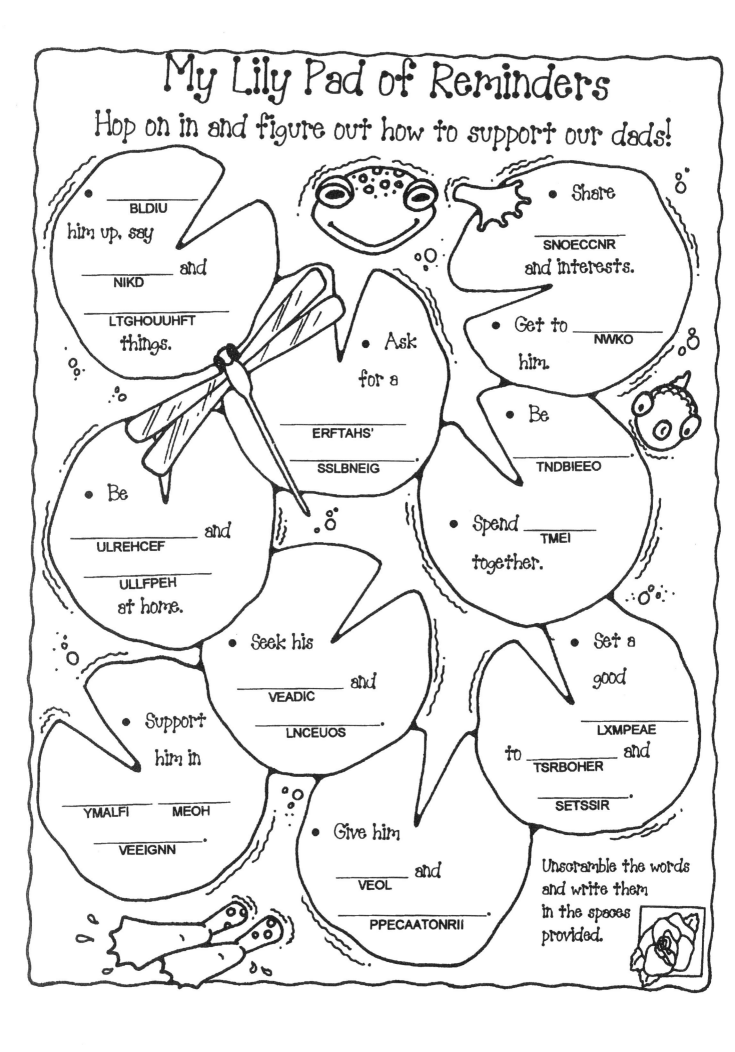

- _____ (BLDIU) him up, say _____ (NIKD) and _____ (LTGHOUUHFT) things.

- Share _____ (SNOECCNR) and interests.

- Get to _____ (NWKO) him.

- Ask for a _____ (ERFTAHS') _____ (SSLBNEIG).

- Be _____ (TNDBIEEO)

- Be _____ (ULREHCEF) and _____ (ULLFPEH) at home.

- Spend _____ (TMEI) together.

- Seek his _____ (VEADIC) and _____ (LNCEUOS).

- Set a good _____ (LXMPEAE) to _____ (TSRBOHER) and _____ (SETSSIR).

- Support him in _____ (YMALFI) _____ (MEOH) _____ (VEEIGNN).

- Give him _____ (VEOL) and _____ (PPECAATONRII).

Unscramble the words and write them in the spaces provided.

Lesson #15	**PRIESTHOOD:** Understanding Melchizedek Priesthood Responsibilities *(Melchizedek Priesthood Seek-n-Match)*

YOU'LL NEED: Copy of Seek-n-Match (page 32) for each young woman, pencils, and markers.

> *Review Discussion (pages 62-63) in Young Women Manual 1*.*

ACTIVITY: Help young women find the scriptures to match the correct responsibilities in the Melchizedek Priesthood Seek-n-Match. The following scriptures describe the offices and responsibilities.

ELDER: D&C 20:39, 41-45, D&C 42:43-44, 80
Answers: B, D, G, H, I, L, O, P, Q
HIGH PRIEST: D&C 20:67 and 107:10;
D&C 84:111 and 68:19
Answers: C, E
PATRIARCH: D&C 107:39-53
Answers: F, J
SEVENTY: D&C 107:25, 34, 38, 93-97
Answers: A, R
APOSTLE: D&C 18:26-27; D&C 107:23, 33
Answers: K, M, N

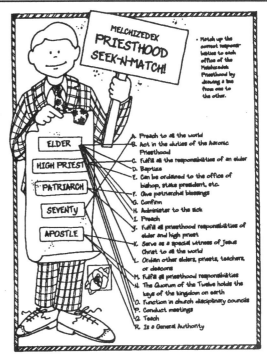

COLOR SYMBOL: Color floral symbol on activity and scripture card. File activity in Young Women Value- able Journal behind value tab.

> *Individual Worth (red rose)*

PERSONAL PROGRESS* GOALS:
Beehive 1 (Individual Worth 3, Knowledge 8)
Mia Maid 1 (Good Works 1)

THOUGHT TREAT: Righteous Roll-ups. Give each young woman a fruit roll-up. Talk about the roles we play in supporting the priesthood. Share your experiences as you have supported them in choosing the right.

MIDWEEK ACTIVITIES:
Future Husband Brainstorm and Priesthood Surprise Package. Have young women write down one characteristic they would like to see in their future husband (on heart-shaped paper).

Put papers in a container and mix them up, then write them on the chalkboard. Discuss what it takes in commitment and dedication to be a worthy Melchizedek Priesthood holder. Discuss what it takes for a young woman to be worthy to marry a Melchizedek Priesthood holder in the temple. Note that these characteristics are the same, and that if the young women desire to marry someone with certain qualities, they must strive to develop these same qualities. End activity by selecting a Melchizedek Priesthood holder in the ward that all young women agree on. Have young women put candy in the container along with the heart-shaped paper with their comments. Decorate the jar and deliver it! Give young women a BIG HUNK candy bar with the following note glued onto bar. (Option: Find bee or heart stickers to place over "bee" and love" on the note below.)

Big hunks aren't necessarily the best. Look for quality and "bee" your best self, and you will "bee" happy and find true happiness and love.

MELCHIZEDEK
PRIESTHOOD
SEEK-N-MATCH!

• Match up the correct responsibilities to each office of the Melchizedek Priesthood by drawing a line from one to the other.

ELDER

HIGH PRIEST

PATRIARCH

SEVENTY

APOSTLE

A. Preach to all the world
B. Act in the duties of the Aaronic Priesthood
C. Fulfill all the responsibilities of an elder
D. Baptize
E. Can be ordained to the office of bishop, stake president, etc.
F. Give patriarchal blessings
G. Confirm
H. Administer to the sick
I. Preach
J. Fulfill all priesthood responsibilities of elder and high priest
K. Serve as a special witness of Jesus Christ to all the world
L. Ordain other elders, priests, teachers, or deacons
M. Fulfill all priesthood responsibilities
N. The Quorum of the Twelve holds the keys of the kingdom on earth
O. Function in church disciplinary councils
P. Conduct meetings
Q. Teach
R. Is a General Authority

Lesson #16	**PRIESTHOOD: I Will Support My Celestial Companion** *(D&C 131:1-4 priesthood support tent card)*

YOU'LL NEED: Copy of priesthood support tent card (page 34) for each young woman, pencils, and markers.

ACTIVITY:
Encourage young women to think ahead

> *Review Thought question (page 66) in Young Women Manual 1*.*

to their eternal marriage relationship and how they might help their companion obtain the highest kingdom. They can support their husband in four ways: motivating, strengthening, sustaining, and guiding.

> *Review Wordstrips and chalkboard discussion (pages 66-67) in Young Women Manual 1*.*

1. Encourage young women to memorize the D&C 131:1-4 scripture on this tent card.
2. Color and cut out tent card, and fold to stand up.
3. Talk about ways they can support priesthood leaders, then give them time to write ways they can support priesthood leaders on the card.

> *Review Chalkboard discussion #1-9 (page 68) in Young Women Manual 1*.*

COLOR SYMBOL: Color floral symbol on activity and scripture card. File activity in Young Women Value-able Journal behind value tab.

> *Individual Worth (red rose)*

PERSONAL PROGRESS* GOALS:
Beehive 2 (Divine Nature 2)
Mia Maid 1 (Divine Nature 8)
Mia Maid 2 (Divine Nature 2)

THOUGHT TREAT: Temple Mints. Tell young women that Heavenly Father "mint" for us to motivate, strengthen, sustain, and guide those we date as well as our eternal companion.

MIDWEEK ACTIVITIES: See Sustaining Priesthood Bearers (Lesson #13) Midweek Activity.

Women and Priesthood Bike-n-Hike. Invite young men to go on a bike and hike. Bike to a park or other location, and surprise young men with a sack lunch. Have young women meet beforehand to prepare two sack lunches, then place lunches in their backpacks along with a tablecloth to spread on the ground. Leaders take the backpacks to the site and place backpacks in the center of a large circle. Young men choose a backpack, find the young woman it belongs to, and enjoy lunch together, sitting on the ground. (But keep this a secret until it's time to eat.)

SACK LUNCH HONOR ROLL (note): Use large rolls for making the sandwiches. Young women can put a note inside the sandwich roll enclosed in a plastic bag for young men to read.

PRIESTHOOD HONOR "ROLL":
This is what I like about a young man who honors his priesthood:

_____

_____

_____

_____   _____
_____   _____
_____   _____
_____   _____

So that I may prepare to partake of
the new and everlasting covenant, I
will support a priesthood holder in the
following ways:

"In the celestial glory there are three
heavens or degrees;
And in order to obtain the highest, a
man must enter into this order of the
priesthood [meaning the new and
everlasting covenant of marriage];
And if he does not, he cannot obtain it.
He may enter into the other, but that is
the end of his Kingdom; he cannot have
an increase.   — D&C 131:1-4

| Lesson #17 | **COVENANTS AND ORDINANCES: I Will Keep Sacred Promises**
(Pick the Path to Eternal Life decision maker) |

YOU'LL NEED: Copy of Pick the Path decision maker (page 36) for each young woman, pencils, and markers.

> *Review Questions and references #1-3 (pages 74-75) in Young Women Manual 1*.*

ACTIVITY: Help young women Pick the Path to Eternal Life by—
1. Reading the scripture references below each stepping stone.
2. Writing in the stone the reward for following each path.
3. Deciding which path you want to follow and color that path.
4. Reading Thought Treat message below.

COLOR SYMBOL: Color floral symbol on activity and scripture card. File activity in Young Women Value-able Journal behind value tab.

> *Divine Nature (blue morning glory)*

PERSONAL PROGRESS* GOALS:
Beehive 2 (Divine Nature 2)
Beehive 2 (Choice & Accountability 7, Integrity 8)
Mia Maid 1 (Faith 3)
Mia Maid 2 (Faith 1, 3, Individual Worth 1, 7)

THOUGHT TREAT: Path Pretzels. Give each young woman a twisted pretzel and straight pretzel. Tell them that the path back to our heavenly home is straight and narrow. If we get off the path and don't repent, life could take many twists and turns that will make it difficult for us to get back on the straight and narrow path that leads to eternal life. By staying focused on making covenants and remaining faithful, we can avoid the twisted pitfalls of life.

MIDWEEK ACTIVITIES:
1. Scripture Situations Search. Search together in the scriptures for various situations when oaths were made and their circumstances. Why were

these oaths made? What were they? Get a feeling for the importance of keeping covenants and promises (see *oaths, covenants, promise, swear, vow,* and *pledge* in the Index and Topical Guide).

2. Object Lesson: "The Lord Never Breaks Covenants." Have two people (a young woman and an adult priesthood holder or bishop) stand together with a metal or paper chain around them. Lock it (or pretend to lock it). Give the key to the young women. Say, "The adult represents the Lord and the young woman is 'you.' You have the power to break a covenant or keep it binding. The Lord can never break a covenant. Only people can." Discuss over ginger snaps or graham crackers and milk how making and keeping covenants makes us strong and extraordinary.

3. Plan a Party After Baptisms for the Dead. Take young women to the temple to be baptized for the dead. Have a special dinner with promise placemats and packages. Talk about the promises we made at our baptism and the promises Heavenly Father makes us in return as we keep our baptismal covenants. Our Promises: to obey the commandments, read the scriptures, honor parents, help others, pay tithing, attend Church meetings. Heavenly Father's Promises: to forgive us when we repent, love and bless us, give us the gift of the Holy Ghost, answer prayers, let us live with him forever.

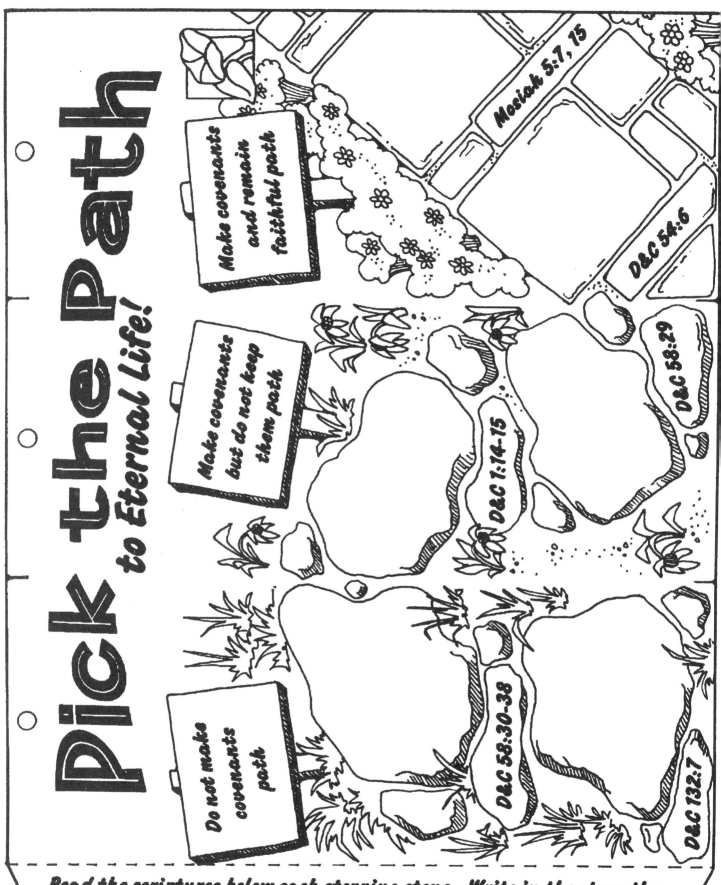

Pick the Path to Eternal Life!

Make covenants and remain faithful path

Mosiah 5:7, 15

D&C 54:6

Make covenants but do not keep them path

D&C 7:14-15

D&C 58:29

Do not make covenants path

D&C 58:30-38

D&C 132:7

Read the scriptures below each stepping stone. Write in the stone the reward for following each path. Decide which path you want to follow.

Lesson #18	**FAMILIES FOREVER:** Temple Marriage Brings Eternal Family Life
	(eternal marriage puzzle quiz)

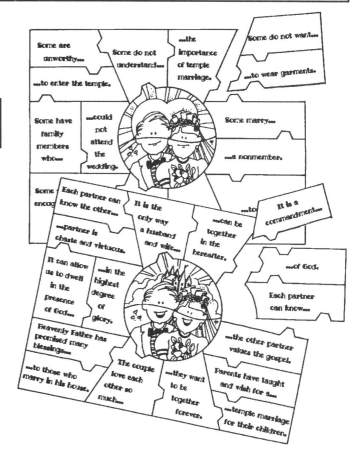

YOU'LL NEED: Copy of puzzles (pages 38-39) and an envelope for each young woman, and markers.

Review Discussion #1-9 (page 77) in Young Women Manual 1*.

ACTIVITY:
1. Color center and cut out two puzzles for each young woman and place in an envelope.
2. Have young women put both puzzles together at the same time, reading the clues that indicate which puzzle it belongs to. The puzzles represent (a) reasons young people give for wanting to marry in the temple, and (b) reasons some do not marry in the temple.
3. Talk about the difference between the brides' and grooms' smiles and the feelings they may have for the choices they make to marry in the temple or outside the temple.

COLOR SYMBOL: Color floral symbol on activity and scripture card. File activity in Young Women Value-able Journal behind value tab.

Individual Worth (red rose)

PERSONAL PROGRESS* GOALS:
Beehive 2 (Divine Nature 2)
Mia Maid 1 (Faith 3, Divine Nature 8)
Mia Maid 2 (Divine Nature 2)

THOUGHT TREAT: Temple Cake. Bake a sheet cake and frost. Cut into squares and place a temple mint on top of each square. As young women enjoy the cake, ask them to think of the sweetness that comes to mind as they imagine themselves married for time and all eternity to the man they will someday come to love.

MIDWEEK ACTIVITIES:
Temple Chase.
Step #1. Get young women together and provide a pleasant setting with temple pictures around the room and/or displayed on tables.
Step #2. Set out the scriptures as well as articles from Church magazines on the temple and eternal marriage. Have groups of young women find scriptures and read articles, etc., to report to the others the various points they discover.
Step #3. Give each young woman a blank sheet of paper and a pen. Have her write down the important points she finds. (Option: Photocopy the temple picture on the following page and reduce it 50% to use as clip-art on this blank sheet of paper.
Step #4. Assign young women group leaders to share what they have learned.
Step #5. Talk about inner strength and how we can resolve to always set our sights on the temple.
Step #6. Discuss appropriate dress and talk about the questions in a recommend interview.

It is a commandment...

...of God.

Each partner can know...

...the other partner values the gospel.

Parents have taught and wish for a...

...temple marriage for their children.

...can be together in the hereafter.

...they want to be together forever.

a husband and wife...

The couple love each other so much...

Each partner can know the other...

It is the only way...

...partner is chaste and virtuous.

...in the highest degree of glory.

It can allow us to dwell in the presence of God...

Heavenly Father has promised many blessings...

...to those who marry in his house.

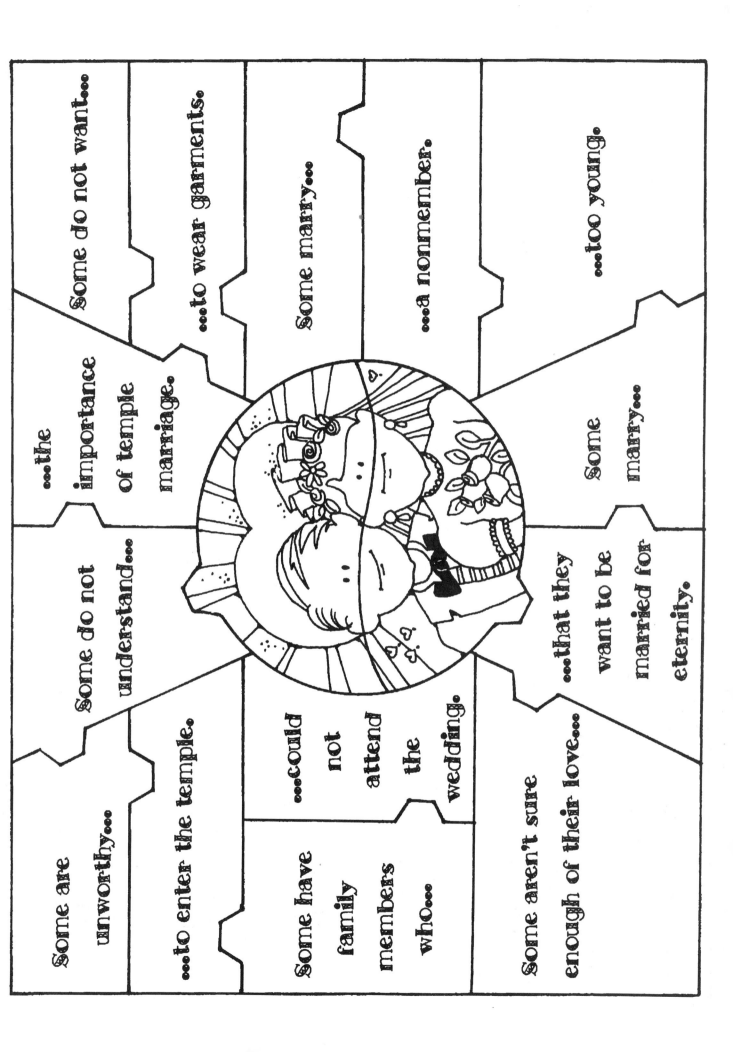

Some do not want... ...to wear garments.

Some marry... ...a nonmember.

...too young.

...the importance of temple marriage.

Some do not understand...

Some marry... that they want to be married for eternity.

Some are unworthy... ...to enter the temple.

Some have family members who... ...could not attend the wedding.

Some aren't sure enough of their love...

Lesson #19	**RECORDS: I Will Make a Personal Record of My Life** *(My Time Line sticker journal)*

YOU'LL NEED: Copy of My Time Line glue-on stickers (page 41), 1 (8 ½ " x 11") sheet of cardstock paper, 16 (8 ½" x 11") sheets of writing paper for each young woman, pencils, and markers.

> *Review Discussion "Why is it important to keep a personal record? How do you know that Heavenly Father wants you to keep a record of your life?" (Page 82) in Young Women Manual 1*.*

ACTIVITY: Use time line glue-on stickers to:
OPTION #1 <u>Create a Personal Time Line Journal</u>. (1) Color and cut out stickers. (2) Glue the My Time Line sticker on cardstock to create the cover for the Time Line journal. (3) Glue a sticker on each of the 16 sheets of writing paper. Respond to each topic, writing your personal history (e.g., give information about your birth below "My Birth" sticker). (4) Add other sheets and drawings. (5) Staple journal pages together.
OPTION #2 <u>Create a Time Line Poster</u> to map out life's events and stories young women wish to put in their journal. Draw a line across the poster from one corner to the other. Glue time line stickers on poster and write key words to indicate points in time. Write about one or two events on the poster and share with class. Continue process at home and obtain ideas from friends and family. Poster can be kept in journal.

COLOR SYMBOL: Color floral symbol on activity and scripture card. File activity in Young Women Value-able Journal behind value tab.

Individual Worth (red rose)

PERSONAL PROGRESS* GOALS:
<u>Beehive 1</u> (Individual Worth 1, 2, 6)
<u>Beehive 2</u> (Individual Worth 1, 2, 7)
<u>Mia Maid 1</u> (Individual Worth 2, 6, 7, Knowledge 8)
<u>Mia Maid 2</u> (Individual Worth 4-8)
<u>Laurel 1 & 2</u> Project #22 (page 79)

THOUGHT TREAT: <u>Journal Scroll Roll-ups</u>. Give each young woman a fruit roll-up. Ask them all to think about their journal as a scroll they roll out and use to write their personal history to share with family, friends, and their future posterity. Ask them to write in their journals consistently to catch life's experiences before the details fade.

MIDWEEK ACTIVITIES:
<u>**Make Covered Photo Albums.**</u>
<u>**Do Some Scrapbooking.**</u>
<u>**Learn About Young Women**</u>. Talk to parents to learn something special in the life of each young woman. Ask for a story about one of the young woman's ancestors (and supply a photo if possible).
<u>**Guess Who? Ancestor and Story Match.**</u>
Put all the photos on the wall and have the young women match the ancestor to the young woman. Read some of the stories and see if anyone can guess whose relative it is. Ask parents for stories the young women don't know about their ancestors. Say, "These experiences are precious, and everything we learn about our ancestors helps us appreciate them more."

My Birth

My Baptism

Jr. High

High School

Toddler

My Family

My Friends

First Day
of School

Age 5

Temple Trips

Favorite
Birthday

Camp

Age 7

My Talents

Vacation

Favorite
Holiday

My Time Line

Lesson #20	**MISSIONARY WORK: I Will Extend My Friendship** *(Light of the Gospel candle gift box)*

YOU'LL NEED: Copy of gift box (page 43), a small birthday cake candle to place in box for each young woman, scissors, glue, and markers.

Review Chalkboard discussion (page 90), Teacher presentation and Testimony (page 91), and Lesson Application (page 92) in Young Women Manual 1*.

I will share my greatest gift... the light of the gospel. Matthew 5:15-16.

1. Become friends with young woman.
2. Invite to Young activities

ACTIVITY: Create a gift candle box ahead of time to present to each young women to remind them of the three steps to sharing their greatest gift—the light of the gospel.
Step #1. Become friends with a young woman.
Step #2. Invite friend to Young Women activities and to church.
Step #3. Invite friend to be taught by the missionaries.
A. Color and cut out box and bow.
B. Fold and glue box together, leaving top flap open.
C. Place a small birthday candle in box.
D. Fold bow on fold lines and glue at the bottom. Slide bow over box.
E. Read Matthew 5:15-16.

COLOR SYMBOL: Color floral symbols on activity and scripture card. File activity in Young Women Value-able Journal behind value tab.

Good Works (yellow sunflower)

PERSONAL PROGRESS* GOALS:
<u>Beehive 1</u> (Faith 3, 5, 8, Divine Nature 3, Choice & Accountability 6, Good Works 8)
<u>Beehive 2</u> (Faith 3, 4, 5, 6, Knowledge 2, Good Works 7, Integrity 7)
<u>Mia Maid 1</u> (Faith 2, 5, Divine Nature 3, Individual Worth 4, 9, Knowledge 6, Integrity 6)
<u>Mia Maid 2</u> (Faith 2, 4, 8, 9, Choice & Accountability 1, 3)
<u>Laurel 1 & 2</u> Projects #5, 19 (page 79)

THOUGHT TREAT: <u>Candle Cookie</u>. Roll out sugar cookie dough and cut dough into candle shapes. Paint cookie dough to look like a burning candle with cookie paints. Mix two teaspoons canned milk with food coloring. Bake cookies. As young women enjoy their cookies, tell them that the more they share the light of the gospel, the more the gospel will mean to them. They will feel more joy when they share the joy that comes from the gospel. (Option: Make more cookies for lesson #21.)

MIDWEEK ACTIVITIES:
<u>Reach Out to Others Humanitarian Projects</u>.
Get together with young men. Give young men the assignment to cut out small wooden blocks or animal shapes that young women can sand and paint. Go around and collect teddy bears and donate to local fire department or police department. Make quilts or collect food donations for homeless shelters. Ask humanitarian representatives in ward or stake, city, or library for ideas. Make sure less active young men and women are brought to this activity. Go out of your way to include all!

I will share my greatest gift... the light of the gospel.

Matthew 5:15-16

1. Become friends with the young woman.

2. Invite friend to Young Women activities and church.

3. Invite friend to meet the missionaries.

Lesson #21	**MISSIONARY WORK: I Will Set a Righteous Example** *(Example Decisions Drama or Draw)*

YOU'LL NEED: Copy of bag label and wordstrips (page 45) a zip-close plastic bag for each young woman, scissors, and markers.

> *Review Chalkboard discussion (page 94) in Young Women Manual 1.*

ACTIVITY: Help young women learn the difference between a positive example of the gospel of Jesus Christ and a negative example.
1. Color and cut out Example Drama or Draw label and wordstrips.
2. Fold label and place inside a plastic bag along with wordstrips.
3. To play, follow instructions on label.
4. Suggest young women share this activity with family and friends, adding more examples.

COLOR SYMBOL: Color floral symbol on activity and scripture card. File activity in Young Women Value-able Journal behind value tab.

> *Choice & Accountability (orange poppy)*

PERSONAL PROGRESS GOALS:
<u>Beehive 1</u> (Faith 3, 5, Choice and Accountability 6, Integrity 3)
<u>Beehive 2</u> (Faith 4-6, Choice & Accountability 1, 7)
<u>Mia Maid 2</u> (Faith 8-9)
<u>Mia Maid 2</u> (Choice & Accountability 3)
<u>Laurel 1 & 2</u> Projects #5, 19 (page 79)

THOUGHT TREAT: <u>Footstep Fudge</u>. Shape fudge like feet and add M&M toes. Ask young women to follow in Jesus' footsteps and be a good example to others.

MIDWEEK ACTIVITIES:
1. **<u>Shining Example Spotlight</u>.** You'll need a flashlight for each young woman, 3 x 5 cards, pencils, and art supplies to make thank-you cards. INVITATION: Ask young women to bring a flashlight and a 1-2 minute spotlight, telling of someone who has been a shining example.

Enjoy activities #1-3 as follows.
Activity #1 Flashlight Spotlight. Start by setting the stage. Turn out the lights and have young women shine their flashlights towards the person giving the spotlight (avoiding their face). Young women can take turns sharing their shining example under the spotlight.
Activity #2 Three Shining Examples. Give each young woman a 3 x 5 card and a pencil to write down three of the shining examples they would like to follow. Before Activity #1, tell young women to listen for three examples they would like to follow.
Activity #3 Thank-You Cards. Using the art supplies, have young women make a homemade thank-you card to send to their shining example.

2. <u>**A Righteous Example Influences Others.**</u> Invite young women to talk about people around them who have set righteous examples for them. Discuss what these individuals have done and why it touched them. What did these individuals do that motivated them to feel stronger or more motivated toward good works? Choose three people young women all agree are righteous examples. Then do something as a group to show these people that you appreciate their example (babysit for them, bake and decorate a "thank-you" cake, or wash their car and vacuum it.) The ideas are endless. Write a note and give Hugs candy along with real hugs.

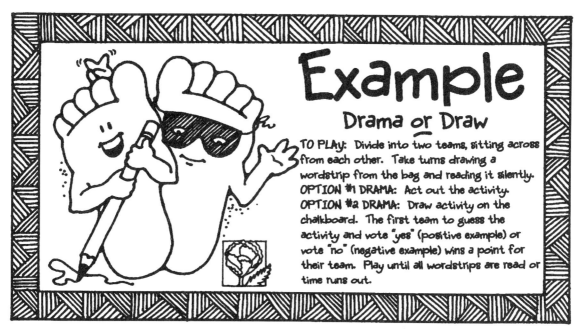

Example
Drama or Draw

TO PLAY: Divide into two teams, sitting across from each other. Take turns drawing a wordstrip from the bag and reading it silently. OPTION #1 DRAMA: Act out the activity. OPTION #2 DRAMA: Draw activity on the chalkboard. The first team to guess the activity and vote "yes" (positive example) or vote "no" (negative example) wins a point for their team. Play until all wordstrips are read or time runs out.

Eat healthy foods	Do the dishes
Modest dress	Drink alcoholic beverages
Immodest dress	Study hard for a test
Visit the sick	Walk and feed the dog
Borrow sunglasses and not return them	Share a candy bar
Go to church	Spend tithing money
Gossip	Pay tithing
Swear	Contribute to the missionary fund
Sluff school	Pay extra on parents' fast offering
Read the scriptures	Drive recklessly

Have family home evening	Disobey parents
Gamble	Come home late
Smoke	Respect country's flag
Watch bad shows	Shoplift
Chose uplifting shows	Write to a missionary
Be kind to children	Be kind to parents
Read to children	Keep room clean
Share your testimony	Shovel snow for a neighbor
Don't swear	Befriend someone who seems alone
Make a meal to surprise your family	Rollerblade across your neighbor's lawn

Read and share an uplifting book	Forget to weed
Read a questionable book and share it	Make a promise and not keep it
Turn bad television programs off	Get up early
Don't tell or listen to dirty jokes	Care for neighbor's house
Do homework	Take your brother or sister to an activity
Copy answers on a test	Don't say thanks
Listen to uplifting music	Make your bed

Lesson #22	**REPENTANCE:** I Will Understand the Worth of Repentance *(Sunshine Repentance doorknob reminder)*

YOU'LL NEED: Copy of Sunshine Repentance doorknob hanger (page 47) on colored cardstock paper for each young woman, scissors, pencils, and markers.

> *Review Scripture Mosiah 27:29 and Steps to Repentance (pages 98-99) and Scripture discussion Alma 36:12-13, 15-16 (page 100) in Young Women Manual 1*.*

ACTIVITY: Young women can create this doorknob hanger as a reminder that repentance helps us to move from darkness into the light.
1. Read the scriptures listed above.
2. Color and cut out doorknob reminder.
3. Fold and glue back to back.
4. Write the steps to repentance found on pages 98-99* as follows: (1) Recognize wrongdoing. (2) Promise never to repeat the sin. (3) Recommit to live the gospel. (4) Make restitution for wrongs: repent in prayer, confess to bishop, apologize to those offended. (5) Feel a depth of repentance as deep as the sin. (6) Prove ourselves worthy over time. (7) Forgive ourselves and those who have offended us. (8) Commit not to look back but accept the Lord's forgiveness.

COLOR SYMBOL: Color floral symbol on activity and scripture card. File activity in Young Women Value-able Journal behind value tab.

> *Choice & Accountability (orange poppy)*

PERSONAL PROGRESS* GOALS:
Beehive 2 (Choice & Accountability 8, Integrity 3)
Mia Maid 2 (Choice & Accountability 7)

THOUGHT TREAT: <u>Fruit Flavored Candies</u>. Tell young women that the warmth of the sun helps fruits and vegetables to grow to their full potential. We too can feel the warmth that comes from repentance, which will help us reach our full potential.

MIDWEEK ACTIVITY:
1. <u>Progress Path</u>. Set up a game in the ward building or a park with a path. Have adult leaders or priesthood helpers, like the bishopric or dads, stand along the path. Create situation cards to be held by the helpers along the path. Have every young woman carry a sturdy sack or backpack. Have them go along the path slowly, picking cards held by the path helpers. For example, the first helper might give a sin card like "Lied to parents about where you were going." The second card might be a repentance card like "Felt feelings of remorse," or "Bore my testimony to a friend." Have helpers put the sin stones (stones with the word "sin" written on them) in their pack as they pass the post. At the few repentance posts, they can take out a stone. The last eight stops are the eight steps of repentance cards, followed by a card with a quote by Spencer W. Kimball (page 100 from the lesson). Take out stones as they pass. Roast marshmallows or have toast and cocoa, and discuss how it feels to get rid of mistakes and recommit, staying on the path that leads to eternal joy.

2. <u>Bring Sunshine into Your Life Workshop</u>. Have young women share ideas on how they can repent and find happiness. IDEAS: Sing a song that will brighten your day, pray often, forgive yourself, forgive others, think of and encourage others, look forward to worthy goals, set priorities, be open to the positive, don't waste time waiting for happiness—give it to yourself.

Sunshine Repentance

Steps to Repentance:

☀ 1. _____
_____

☀ 2. _____
_____

☀ 3. _____
_____

☀ 4. _____
_____

☀ 5. _____
_____

☀ 6. _____
_____

☀ 7. _____
_____

☀ 8. _____
_____

I can move from darkness to the light and feel the warmth and peace that true repentance brings!

Mosiah 27:29

Lesson #23	**FORGIVENESS: I Will Forgive Others**
	(Ephesians 4:32 bite-size memorize poster)

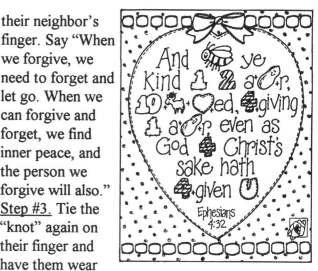

YOU'LL NEED: Copy of bite-size memorize poster (page 49) and markers for each young woman. (Option: Make an enlarged copy of the poster for presentation.)

Review Preparation #2 (page 101) and Poster presentation (page 103) in Young Women Manual 1*.

ACTIVITY:
1. Color and memorize this Ephesians 4:32 bite-size memorize poster to help young women learn the importance of forgiving others.
2. Role-play forgiving situations. Divide young women into two groups to role-play situations where forgiveness is needed and how the other person forgives.
3. Talk about how a situation they might turn out if someone did not forgive. How would they feel in days, weeks, months, and years to come?

COLOR SYMBOL: Color floral symbol on activity and scripture card. File activity in Young Women Value-able Journal behind value tab.

Individual Worth (red rose)

PERSONAL PROGRESS* GOALS:
Beehive 1 (Divine Nature 3)
Mia Maid 1 (Choice & Accountability 6)

THOUGHT TREAT: Gingerbread Men. Remind young women that we are to forgive all men. Read Matthew 6:14 *"For if ye forgive men their trespasses, your heavenly Father will also forgive you."* Imagine how you would feel if Heavenly Father did not forgive you. Others may feel the same when until we forgive them.

MIDWEEK ACTIVITIES:
1. Forgive and Forget-me-"knot".
Step #1. Give each young woman an 8-inch piece of string and ask someone to tie it on her finger with a "knot." Say, "When we don't forgive others, our spirit gets tied up in 'knots' and our spirit isn't free to love that person."
Step #2. Ask young women to untie the "knot" on

their neighbor's finger. Say "When we forgive, we need to forget and let go. When we can forgive and forget, we find inner peace, and the person we forgive will also." Step #3. Tie the "knot" again on their finger and have them wear the string home as a reminder "knot" to forget to forgive others.

2. Forgiving Hearts, Letting Go! Have young women write on a heart shaped note something they are truly willing to let go of (a hurt, bad feelings about someone, etc.). Discuss how when we don't forgive, our heart and mind cannot move onto more important things. Forgiveness frees our spirit, leaving room for love and friendship. Have each young woman tie her note to a helium balloon and let it go, letting go of the hurt and bad feeling. Serve heart shaped cookies with "forgiving heart" written on each, and a glass of strawberry flavored milk with strawberry ice cubes (freeze strawberry milk in ice cube trays).

3. Red Rose Peace Offering. Say, "The yellow hybrid tea rose is known as the symbol of peace. It was smuggled in from France in 1942 and given out at the United Nations meeting in 1945 that marked the end of the war." Give each young woman the following note to give a friend or family member. Color the rose yellow.

This rose represents my friendship and love. It represents peace.
I'm sorry if I have ever offended you or mistreated you. I love you.
Love, _____

Lesson #24	**PRAYER:** I Value Daily Prayer and Meditation *(Heavenly Phone Call crossmatch)*

YOU'LL NEED: Copy of crossmatch (page 51) for each young woman, pencils, and markers.

> *Review Chalkboard activity #1-10 (page 108) in Young Women Manual 1*.*

ACTIVITY: Tell young women that "a simple phone call can be made each day to Heavenly Father." Use Heavenly Phone Call crossmatch activity to learn how prayer will help. Draw a line from the column on the left to matching words in the column on the right.

ANSWERS: Say "Prayers will help us build a testimony, overcome negative attitudes, observe a meaningful fast, withstand peer group pressures, maintain Church standards, solve school problems, improve one's self-image, keep the Word of Wisdom, develop good habits, and overcome weaknesses."

COLOR SYMBOL: Color floral symbol on activity and scripture card. File activity in Young Women Value-able Journal behind value tab.

> *Faith (white lily)*

PERSONAL PROGRESS* GOALS:
Beehive 1 (Faith 6)
Beehive 2 (Faith 7, Individual Worth 6)
Mia Maid 1 (Faith 4)

THOUGHT TREAT: <u>Prayer Memory Mints</u>. Give each young woman a bag of mints with this reminder note:

Heavenly Father "mint" for us to pray to him each day."

MIDWEEK ACTIVITIES:
1. **Meditation Moments.** Find a special place, (a park, mountain stream, beautiful meadow) away from crowds. (In the winter go to a

beautiful place.) Dress warm. Have young women listen for several minutes without speaking, then discuss the silence. Ask, "When was the last time you did something like this?" Talk about distractions (e.g., TV, radio, cars, people, children, etc.). Express the importance of meditation and prayer. Ask if Joseph Smith could have received his first vision in his home, a house full of people coming and going. Express the importance of meditating, and listening to the Spirit for inspiration and answers.

2. **"Chew"s Something to Pray About.** Have young women sit in a circle in front of a bowl of gum balls or sticks of gum (with at least three pieces of gum for each and a variety of gum—bubble gum, gum balls, sugar-free, etc.) Ask young women to meditate a few moments on things they like to pray about, then write at least three things they like to pray about on three slips of paper and place these in the center in another bowl. Ask young women to take turns drawing a wordstrip out of the bowl and reading what the other young women like to pray about. If someone chooses a wordstrip with an idea that she wrote, she hands the note to a leader to read and chooses a piece of gum. Several young women may have had the same idea and can also choose a piece of gum. If their idea comes up again, they can have another piece of gum. Keep going until all wordstrips are read.

Heavenly Phone Call Crossmatch

A simple phone call can be made each day to Heavenly Father. Prayer will help in:

Overcoming	the Word of Wisdom
Keeping	a testimony
Withstanding	negative attitudes
Developing	weaknesses
Observing	a meaningful fast
Building	school problems
Solving	my self-image
Improving	Church standards
Maintaining	peer group pressure
Overcoming	good habits

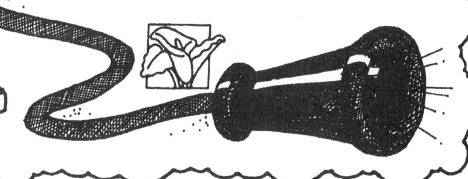

Lesson #25	**SABBATH DAY: I Will Choose Worthy Sabbath Activities** *(Sabbath Day Planner)*

YOU'LL NEED: Copy of Sabbath Day Planner (page 53) for each young woman, pencils, and markers.

> *Review Writing activity and Group brainstorm (page 109) in Young Women Manual 1*.*

ACTIVITY: Ask young women to think of how they are measuring up to Sabbath day activities. Are the activities doing good? Are they spiritually uplifting? Would Jesus do these activities on the Sabbath?
1. Color planner.
2. Write what you can do on Saturday to prepare for the Sabbath.
3. Write activities you will do on Sunday that keep the Sabbath day holy.

COLOR SYMBOL: Color floral symbol on activity and scripture card. File activity in Young Women Value-able Journal behind value tab.

> *Choice & Accountability (orange poppy)*

PERSONAL PROGRESS* GOALS:
Beehive 1 (Choice & Accountability 4)
Beehive 2 (Faith 1, Individual Worth 6, Choice & Accountability 1, Integrity 6)
Mia Maid 1 (Choice & Accountability 4)
Mia Maid 2 (Faith 7, Integrity 1)

THOUGHT TREAT: 7th Day 7 Candy Reminder. Give each young woman 7 candies, e.g., M&Ms. Have them eat 5 pieces of candy. As they eat #6, have them tell something they can do to prepare for the Sabbath. As they eat #7, have them name a worthy Sabbath day activity.

MIDWEEK ACTIVITIES:
1. **Make a Sabbath Day Quiet Book for Children.** Invite someone who does quiet books to come with supplies to show young women how to make them. Girls can give books to a charity, donate them to a ward family or the nursery, or

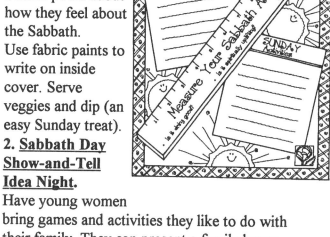

save them for their own children someday. Have young women write a short poem about how they feel about the Sabbath. Use fabric paints to write on inside cover. Serve veggies and dip (an easy Sunday treat).

2. **Sabbath Day Show-and-Tell Idea Night.**
Have young women bring games and activities they like to do with their family. They can present a family home evening idea, gospel game (or any game their family enjoys), scripture activities, and more.
SABBATH DAY IDEAS: Bible Bingo (make up your own game), scripture chase, sharing time lessons from the *Friend*, thumbprint pictures using animals found in the scriptures; share journal entries, review missionary discussions, write letters to missionaries or family and friends, celebrate the birth of Jesus (with a birthday party), tell stories about ancestors or about an ancestor's possession with show-and-tell, make a gospel grab bag by looking up favorite scriptures and placing them in a bag (young women can draw them out of a bag and try to guess the young woman who wrote the scripture). Young women can also make a testimony time capsule by writing testimonies, burying them in a container, and digging them up before graduating from the Young Women program. With these ideas and those of your young women, you should be able to make each Sabbath day memorable.
3. **Thought Treat Sharing and Tasting Table.**
Have young women bring a treat and relate it the gospel like the Thought Treat on the left or the hundreds of other Thought Treats in the Ross and King books.

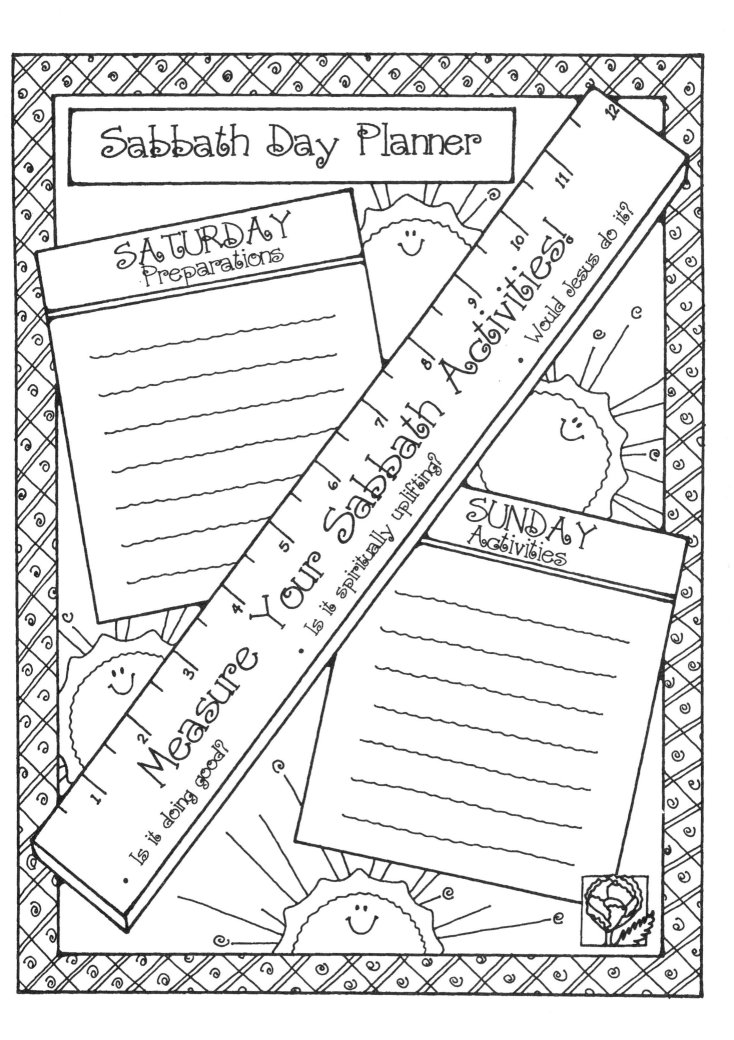

Lesson #26	**TESTIMONY: I Will Strengthen and Share My Testimony**
	(My Testimony Seeds packet with scripture clues)

YOU'LL NEED: Copy of seed packet (page 55) and seeds for each young woman, scissors, glue, scriptures, pencils, and markers.

Review Preparation #2 (page 113) and Scripture activity and discussion (page 114) in Young Women Manual 1*.

ACTIVITY:
1. Color and cut out seed packet and wordstrips.
2. Fold packet in half and glue back to back 1/4-inch on the sides and bottom only, leaving the top open.
3. Fill seed packet with a few seeds (flowers or vegetables) to be planted. Challenge young women to think, as they plant and nourish the seeds, about how they can plant and nourish their testimony.
4. Read the scriptures and write what is necessary to gain and nourish a testimony.

COLOR SYMBOL: Color floral symbol on activity and scripture card. File activity in Young Women Value-able Journal behind value tab.

Faith (white lily)

PERSONAL PROGRESS* GOALS:
Beehive 1 (Faith 7, Knowledge 7)
Beehive 2 (Faith 4, 6, 8, Knowledge 2, Choice & Accountability 7)
Mia Maid 1 (Faith 5, 6, Knowledge 6, Integrity 8)
Mia Maid 2 (Faith 4-6, Individual Worth 8, Knowledge 2-3, 6, Integrity 6)
Laurel 1 & 2 Projects #7, 8 (page 79)

THOUGHT TREAT: Sunflower Seeds. Place sunflower seeds inside seed packet for activity detailed above.

MIDWEEK ACTIVITIES:
1. **Testimony Match Game.** Give young women two wordstrips and ask them to write a part, or a phrase, of their testimony on one wordstrip. Then have them write it again on the second wordstrip. Have them divide into two teams and play concentration by turning over two wordstrips to make a match. When a match is made, post one of each pair of wordstrips on the board or a poster. Afterwards, have young women take turns reading a testimony wordstrip and adding their own feelings to that testimony.

2. **Sharing Time Testimony Meeting.** Have young women each present a short testimony to the Primary children during sharing time. Have young women create visuals or find visuals from the ward library that help them share their testimony. Their testimony might be on a gospel principle they feel strongly about (e.g., tithing, choosing the right, baptism, forgiveness, the Prophet Joseph Smith, Jesus Christ, the Holy Ghost, repentance, the Articles of Faith, Atonement, blessings, priesthood, faith, missionary work, sacrament, the Word of Wisdom).

3. **Testimony Tracker.** Have young women create a special notebook they can take to church meetings or put by their bed to note testimony ideas. As they learn of others' testimonies, ask them to try living certain gospel principles to increase their testimony. Say, "As you do this, record experiences that helped your testimony grow in this Testimony Tracker notebook."

4. **Testimony Meeting Under the Stars.** Gather young women together and give them a piece of paper. Have them write their names on the paper, then show an appropriate church video that expresses what the Church is about (e.g., a video on the Savior or Joseph Smith and the Restoration). Afterwards, allow the young women to go to separate places and for 15 minutes write their feelings about the gospel. Tell them to write exactly what they feel. If they do not feel they are certain about gospel truths, ask them to write what they feel and know. Then gather the papers and read them without giving names (return them later). Help young women know they do have testimonies, some just beginning, others larger. Express that the size does not matter as much as the striving to know, grow, and continuing to nourish it. Express your own testimony and love for them. If possible, go to where you can all lie down on a blanket and look at the stars (or do something else that is inspiring). Pass out "starbursts" candy or other treat to reinforce the grand scheme of creation and our Heavenly Father's power and love.

fold and glue

To gain a testimony I must:

❀ (Alma 5:46) _____

❀ (Alma 32:27) _____

❀ (D&C 11:22) _____

❀ (Moroni 10:4) _____

❀ (John 7:17) _____

Testimony Seeds

I can know for myself that
Jesus is the Christ, that
Joseph Smith is a prophet
and that the Church is true if
I choose to nourish the
testimony seeds within me.

fold and glue

Lesson #27	**SCRIPTURES: I Will Study the Scriptures Daily** *(Search and Ponder bookmark)*

YOU'LL NEED: Copy of bookmark (page 57) on colored cardstock paper for each young woman, pencils, and markers.

> *Review Preparation #4 (page 117), Teacher presentation #1-5 (page 119), and Handout (page 120) in Young Women Manual 1*.*

ACTIVITY: Help young women review the steps to make scripture reading more meaningful. Color and cut out bookmark. Ask young women to try following these steps each day for one week and share their experiences the following week.

COLOR SYMBOL: Color floral symbol on activity and scripture card. File activity in Young Women Value-able Journal behind value tab.

> *Knowledge (green ivy)*

PERSONAL PROGRESS* GOALS:
Beehive 1 (Knowledge 6, Choice & Accountability 2, 7)
Beehive 2 (Faith 4, Divine Nature 1, Knowledge 2)
Mia Maid 1 (Good Works 3, Integrity 8)
Mia Maid 2 (Good Works 4)
Laurel 1 & 2 Project #6 (page 79)

THOUGHT TREAT: Heart Shaped Cookies. Tell young women that each time they read the scriptures, their hearts and minds can feel the Spirit of the Holy Ghost as it speaks to our hearts and minds, letting us know truth.

MIDWEEK ACTIVITIES:
1. Bite-size Memorize Scripture Posters. Provide paper or cardstock for each young woman. Ask her to select a favorite scripture and create a bite-size memorize poster using rebus messages (see Lesson #23 Ephesians 4:32 bite-size memorize poster). The more pictures drawn the better. Have young women share their bite-size memorize posters to see if the other young women can read it. Encourage them to memorize their scripture.
2. Scripture Books Spelling Bee. Have young women write the names of the books on slips of paper and place them in a container. Divide into two teams, and have someone read the names as teams take turns spelling them. The team with the most points after a

designated time wins.
If time is up and all the names of the books have been spelled, place them back in the container to guess again.
3. Scripture Seek and Run.
Create a challenging scripture game where young women search the scriptures in teams and run to find clues taped to the walls before time is up.
TO MAKE GAME: Before activity, have young women class presidents and leaders get together. Search the scriptures together and write questions on slips of paper.
On a separate paper, write clues that provide the answers (to be taped to walls around the activity room.) Sample Question: In 1 Nephi 13:9, what destroys the saints of God and brings them down into captivity? Clue card: "the _ _ _ _ _ _ of the world." The answer and missing word is "praise of the world."
TO PLAY: You'll need a watch with a second hand. Divide young women into teams and take turns drawing a question. Each team has 1 minute to find the scripture and the clue taped to the wall. If they can't do this, the other team has 1 minute to find the answer. If the second team can't find it, the first team tries again. The team with the most clue cards completed win.
RULES: The one-minute time starts after the question is read. The team that is not participating does not open their scriptures until it is their turn. Scriptures must be closed at the beginning of each question. Write in a few missing words as a clue after 1 minute time is up.
3. Surprise Scripture Cupcakes. Wrap a Book of Mormon scripture question with the reference in foil, and insert it inside a cupcake (with a knife after baking or drop into batter before baking). Frost cupcakes and as young women eat them, they will find a surprise question inside. (Supply wet wipes.) After eating, have young women find the answers to their cupcake questions in the scriptures. Choose pertinent scriptures about heros, e.g., Abinidi, Alma the younger's conversion, Nephi's obedience. Have young women read and discuss their questions. (Option: Young women can team up and discuss questions first). Liken their experiences to our day. Tell young women that just as they found scriptures in their cupcakes, they can find answers to life's questions in the scriptures.

Search & Ponder

"For my soul delighteth in the scriptures and my ♥ pondereth them."
-2 Nephi 4:15

As I read the scriptures, I will...

1. Start with prayer.
2. Have paper and pencil ready.
3. Take my time.
4. Ask questions as I read.
5. Stop and ponder.

Search & Ponder

"For my soul delighteth in the scriptures and my ♥ pondereth them."
-2 Nephi 4:15

As I read the scriptures, I will...

1. Start with prayer.
2. Have paper and pencil ready.
3. Take my time.
4. Ask questions as I read.
5. Stop and ponder.

| **Lesson #28** | **TEMPTATION: I Must Be Strong to Resist Temptation** *(Temptation Traps and Escapes brainstorm)* |

YOU'LL NEED: Copy of Temptation Trap cards (pages 59-61) for each young woman and an envelope to store cards, pencils, and markers.

Review Chalkboard and Group activity (page 123) in Young Women Manual 1*.

ACTIVITY: Cut out a set of cards and stack in front of young women face down. Ask young women to divide into groups of 3 or 4 girls. Have them draw two or more <u>Temptation Trap</u> cards. Discuss with your group and write on the card the <u>Escape Route,</u> how they can overcome or combat that temptation. Report your discussion and Escape Route to the class.

COLOR SYMBOL: Color floral symbol on activity and scripture card. File activity in Young Women Value-able Journal behind value tab.

Choice & Accountability (orange poppy)

PERSONAL PROGRESS* GOALS:
<u>Beehive 1</u> (Integrity 1, 2)
<u>Beehive 2</u> (Choice & Accountability 2, 5, 7, 8, Integrity 7)

THOUGHT TREAT: <u>Box Cookies</u>. Frost graham crackers together to create a Box Cookie for each young woman. Tell young women that sin makes people feel boxed in, making it difficult for them to feel free. As we repent and avoid temptation traps, we exercise our right to the free agency Jesus and Heavenly Father want us to have. If we think ahead, we can avoid being trapped by those who feel trapped themselves. Read 3 Nephi 18:18-21.

MIDWEEK ACTIVITIES:
1. <u>Temptation Weight Lifting</u>. Have young women bring some weights (or two cans of soup) and have a weight lifting class. Discuss the weight Satan puts upon us if we accept his temptations. We have the power to push on through any temptation if we "hearken unto the word of God . . . . The fiery darts of the adversary will not overpower us unto blindness or lead us to destruction" (1 Nephi 15:24).
2. <u>Knowledge Is Power</u>. Ask young women what their Achilles' heal is (their vulnerable or weak spot).

See Story (page 122) in lesson*. Discuss common Achilles' heels. Be willing to share yours as a leader. Mention that there are some we need not share but we should know what they are. Discuss the idea that "knowledge is power." If we know we have a weakness, we can best combat it. Discuss some of the weaknesses brought up and what might be done to avoid them. Have someone come who has been successful at overcoming her Achilles' heel (a major problem) who would be willing to share (e.g., drug abuse, smoking, anger, addiction to soap operas, etc.).

3. <u>White Balloon Bounce and Black Balloon Stomp</u>. Give each young woman a white and a black balloon to blow up and tie. Tell young women that the white balloon represents purity and the ability to resist temptation and the black balloon represents temptation.

<u>Step #1.</u> (White Balloon Bounce): Have young women think of one or two ways they can resist temptation and write it on everyone's balloon with permanent marker. Have young women at the same time bounce their balloons into the air, giving an idea on how to resist temptation, e.g., obey parents, dress modestly, come home from dates early, get enough rest, read the scriptures, pray, attend church, serve others, listen to the Spirit of the Holy Ghost, read the *Era,* listen to the prophet. Girls can take balloons home.

<u>Step #2.</u> (Black Balloon Stomp): Tell young women that we can "help" each other stomp out temptation by being a good example and sharing the gospel. Give young women a 12-inch string to tie the black balloon to their ankle (with shoes off). At "go," everyone tries to stomp on their neighbor's temptation balloon. When the balloon is popped, she can leave the stomp. The last person with a balloon says, "Help!" and the others can rush back in to stomp out her temptation (balloon).

Temptation Trap:

Shoplifting

Escape Route:

Temptation Trap:

Deception

Escape Route:

Temptation Trap:

Drinking

Escape Route:

Temptation Trap:

Disobedience to
Parents

Escape Route:

Temptation Trap:

Breaking the
Sabbath

Escape Route:

Temptation Trap:

Taking Drugs

Escape Route:

Temptation Trap:

Bad Music

Escape Route:

_____
_____
_____
_____
_____
_____
_____

Temptation Trap:

Bad Movies

Escape Route:

_____
_____
_____
_____
_____
_____
_____

Temptation Trap:

Evil Speaking of Others

Escape Route:

_____
_____
_____
_____
_____
_____
_____

Temptation Trap:

Laziness

Escape Route:

_____
_____
_____
_____
_____
_____
_____

Temptation Trap:

Unchaste Behavior

Escape Route:

_____
_____
_____
_____
_____
_____
_____

Temptation Trap:

Selfishness

Escape Route:

_____
_____
_____
_____
_____
_____
_____

Temptation Trap:

Lying

Escape Route:

_____

_____

_____

_____

_____

_____

_____

_____

Temptation Trap:

Cheating

Escape Route:

_____

_____

_____

_____

_____

_____

_____

_____

Temptation Trap:

Profanity

Escape Route:

_____

_____

_____

_____

_____

_____

_____

_____

Temptation Trap:

Stealing

Escape Route:

_____

_____

_____

_____

_____

_____

_____

_____

Temptation Trap:

Procrastination

Escape Route:

_____

_____

_____

_____

_____

_____

_____

_____

Temptation Trap:

Discouragement

Escape Route:

_____

_____

_____

_____

_____

_____

_____

_____

Lesson #29

SECOND COMING: I Will Prepare for the Coming of Jesus
(D&C 87:8 tent card with Second Coming preparation list)

YOU'LL NEED: Copy of tent card (page 63) for each young woman, scissors, pencils, and markers.

Review Quotation (page 125) in Young Women Manual 1*.

ACTIVITY: Help young women know they are special and have a special purpose in preparing for the second coming of Jesus with this activity:
1. Color and cut out tent card.
2. Read quote by H. Burke Peterson on the tent card and encourage young women to notice in their lives when they feel Heavenly Father's presence (as they make their journey in life).
3. Write on the card what they can do to prepare for the Second Coming.
4. Tell young women that if they go the extra mile by showing service, they are serving the Savior as well, walking in his steps.

COLOR SYMBOL: Color floral symbol on activity and scripture card. File activity in Young Women Value-able Journal behind value tab.

Integrity (purple pansy)

PERSONAL PROGRESS* GOALS:
<u>Beehive 1</u> (Faith 4)
<u>Beehive 2</u> (Faith 4, Integrity 4)

THOUGHT TREAT: <u>Second Coming Crunch</u>. Give each young woman a granola bar and this note to remind them to help others to prepare:

SECOND COMING CRUNCH
Munch on this crunchy bar and think how you can help those who are in a crunch and need help.
By doing this, you will also receive assistance when you are in a crunch.
This act of service will help you prepare for the Second Coming.

MIDWEEK ACTIVITIES:
1. <u>Service Project of Preparation</u>. Invite several young children to your home for a few hours to play games, hear stories, and do a craft to give some much needed rest to moms or dads in your ward. After parents leave with children, have young women express (1) how it felt to serve, (2) how it felt to be with children, (3) how they can prepare for the Second Coming by doing the most important things.

2. <u>Second Coming Balloon Send-off!</u> Have a helium-filled balloon for each young woman with a <u>string attached</u> (not a ribbon). Ask young women to notice the <u>string attached</u> to this balloon. Tell them that Jesus Christ gave us two gifts unconditionally with "<u>no strings attached</u>," hoping that we would give our gifts to him "<u>with no strings attached</u>." He suffered for our sins so that we could repent. He was crucified, and resurrected so that all men might live again. His plan is for us to live with him again. He did this because he loves us and wants us to have the blessings of eternal life. We can thank him for sacrificing for these gifts by living the commandments, repenting, and following in his steps. We can do this with "<u>no strings attached</u>" (showing our unconditional love) through service, keeping the commandments, and sharing the gospel with others. This way we can obtain the gift we want to earn, the gift with a "<u>string attached</u>," the gift of eternal life, so we will be ready when he comes again. Have young women write a thank-you letter on their balloon, thanking the Savior for his sacrifice and telling how they will prepare for his return. Take turns reading the letters. Ask young women to untie the string and all at the same time let their balloons go! Take photos of this event for young women to remember this moment and to look forward to Christ's second coming.

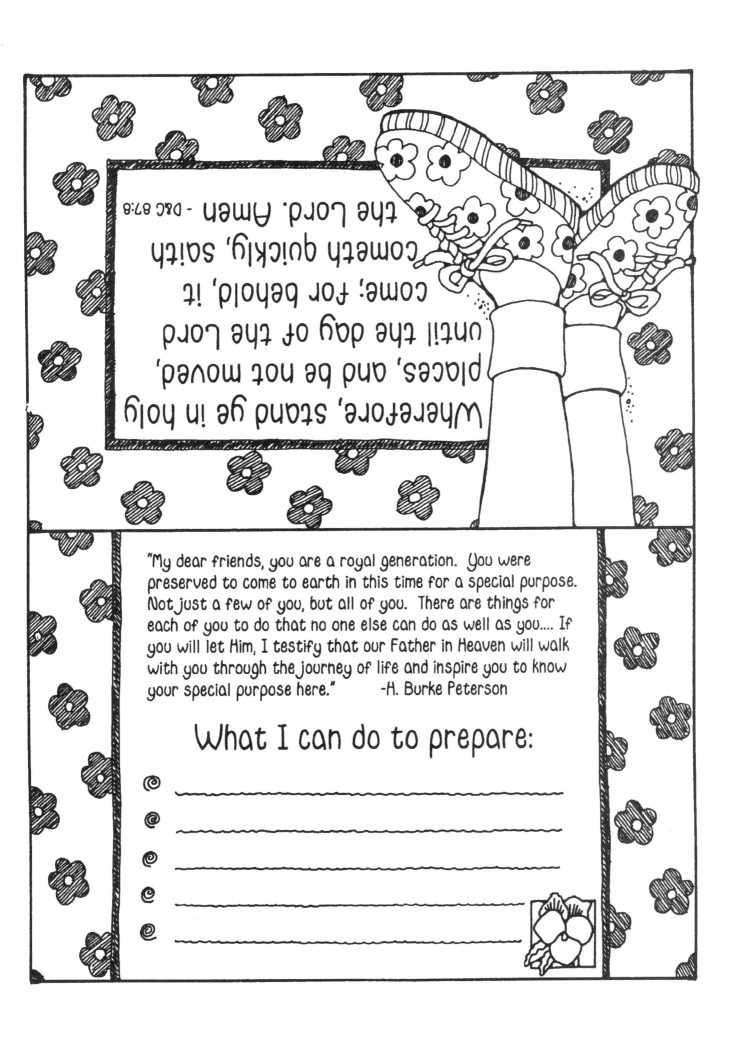

Wherefore, stand ye in holy places, and be not moved, until the day of the Lord come; for behold, it cometh quickly, saith the Lord. Amen. - D&C 87:8

"My dear friends, you are a royal generation. You were preserved to come to earth in this time for a special purpose. Not just a few of you, but all of you. There are things for each of you to do that no one else can do as well as you.... If you will let Him, I testify that our Father in Heaven will walk with you through the journey of life and inspire you to know your special purpose here."   -H. Burke Peterson

What I can do to prepare:

© _____

© _____

© _____

© _____

© _____

Lesson #30	**SERVICE: I Will Find Joy in Service** *(Serve with Style fashionable match game)*

YOU'LL NEED: Copy two sets of match cards (pages 65-66) for each young woman, and markers.

Review Scripture (page 131) in Young Women Manual 1*.

ACTIVITY: To help young women understand what attitude is best when giving service, Introduce the game by reading the card set: "You can be fashionable without spending a dime [card 1] and serve with a smile time after time [card 2]." Read 2 Corinthians 9:7. Then play match game. Matches read left to right.
TO MAKE: Color and cut out card sets.
TO PLAY: Divide into teams and sit in a circle around a table. Lay cards face down on the table. Have young women sit in a circle and take turns drawing a card to make a match. Award winning team with extra candy (see Thought Treat below).

COLOR SYMBOL: Color floral symbols on activity and scripture card. File activity in Young Women Value-able Journal behind value tab.

Good Works (yellow sunflower)

PERSONAL PROGRESS* GOALS:
Beehive 1 (Individual Worth 6, Knowledge 3, Good Works 1, 2, 3, 5, 7, 8, 9)
Beehive 2 (Individual Worth 6, Knowledge 3, 4, Good Works 2, 3, 5, 6, Individual Worth 1)
Mia Maid 1 (Individual Worth 4, Knowledge 5, 9, Good Works 2, 4-7)
Mia Maid 2 (Knowledge 8, Good Works 1-3, 5-8)
Laurel 1 & 2 Projects #2, 4, 12-18, 20 (page 79)

THOUGHT TREAT: Bit-o-Honey Candy.
Give each young woman a Bit-o-Honey candy bar and say:

Service is sweet, so buzz on over to serve someone this week.

MIDWEEK ACTIVITIES:
1. Service Sing-along. Copy songs from the *Hymns** and frame them with borders. Have Young Women place them in their notebook behind the Good Works divider tab. Look for songs on page 425 under the "Service" topic. (For example, "Because I Have Been Given Much," page 219, or "Scatter Sunshine," page 230.)
2. Service Inventions. Drive young women around the neighborhood and assign someone to take notes. List all they see that could be a service project. It's important that the girls do the noticing and noting. Go back to church or home, and decide which is most needful. Make assignments and plan the project(s), e.g., time and equipment needed and permission (if needed). Let the bishop know of the plan, and decide if they should keep it anonymous or not, and who should do what. Let young women lead on this; you sit back and advise a little. When it's their idea, the desire to serve is greater and the less you will need to motivate.

Top off your day with prayer...

Skirt pride and selfishness...

Polish up your talents...

...and remember those that need special blessings.

...and forget yourself and listen to others.

...and share with others what your fingers can do.

Curl up in a chair with a child...

Hats off to Mom and all she does...

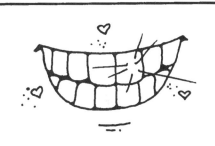

Brush up your pearly whites...

...and read them a good book.

...give her a day off household chores.

...and share your smile with the lonely.

You can be fashionable without spending a dime...

Cinch up your belt for fast Sunday...

 Roll up your sleeves...

...and serve with a smile time after time. (2 Cor. 9:7)

...and prepare the after-fast meal ahead of time!

...and do an extra batch of dishes.

Get your socks to hop to it...

Slip into a new habit...

 Boot yourself out of bed...

...and serve by running an errand.

...and serve someone new each week.

...and make your family a surprise breakfast.

	DATING: I Will Develop Friendships Through Wholesome Group Activities
Lesson #31	*(Group Troupers! Activity Ideas notepad)*

YOU'LL NEED: Copy two or three Group Troupers notepad forms (page 68) for each young woman, pencils, and markers.

> *Review Brainstorming (pages 136-137) in Young Women Manual 1*.*

ACTIVITY: Use these Group Troupers! Activity Ideas pages as a notepad to write wholesome ideas suggested by young women. See Brainstorm ideas in the lesson: make your own movie, write your own books, or put on your own theater; take children on an outing (e.g., the zoo, a formal dinner, or to visit hospitals or shut-ins), walk the dog, watch a ball game, take a bus ride; go bike riding, bowling, swimming, ice skating, dancing, or roller skating; play bingo, board games (e.g., Monopoly), or card games (e.g., Skipbo); have a holiday, birthday, family party, or a picnic; cook or take a cooking class, plan a garage sale or a service project, walk in the park, read books to children, read a favorite book together, plant or weed a garden. Hold a sports competition.

COLOR SYMBOL: Color floral symbol on activity and scripture card. File activity in Young Women Value-able Journal behind value tab.

> *Choice & Accountability (orange poppy)*

PERSONAL PROGRESS* GOALS:
Beehive 2 (Choice & Accountability 2)
Beehive 2 (Integrity 7)
Mia Maid 2 (Choice & Acc. 1-2, Integrity 1)
Mia Maid 2 (Integrity 3-4)

THOUGHT TREAT: M&M Ice Cream Cones. For each activity the young women suggest, give them an M&M to place on their ice cream cone. Suggest that each time they see an M&M candy, they think of a wholesome activity they can do with dates, friends, and family.

MIDWEEK ACTIVITIES:
1. Host a Dance. Young women can host a theme dance with the works (dance instructors, food, and disc jockey).
Dance Theme #1 Western (square dance, line dancing, or swing; have Kentucky Fried Chicken box lunches, apple bobbing, bales of hay, and western wear).
Dance Theme #2 Ballroom (dress formal; have a formal dinner).
Dance Theme #3 Fifties (dance 50s oldies, e.g., Beatles, Beach Boys, Elvis, Jan and Dean; have hamburgers, fries, malts with whipped cream and a cherry on top).
Dance Theme #4 Disco Fever (disco and Grease music, with a John Travolta and Olivia Newton-John dancing contest; have pizza, root beer floats).
Dance and Movie Theme #5 Roaring Twenties (show the movie *Thoroughly Modern Millie* and make raspberry ice cream because in the movie Millie's friend says "raspberries!"). To make ice cream mix vanilla ice cream with frozen raspberries, adding milk as you blend in a blender.
AT ALL DANCES: Have instructors present to teach dance steps. Give boys even numbers and girls odd numbers and place them in a drawing bowl for girls and one for boys. Have the girls draw a boy's number to choose a partner, and then boys choose a girl's number the next time. Let them choose a partner for a contest and award prizes.
2. Pie Eating Contest. Have young women bake pies and young men compete to eat them. Then serve pies with ice cream on top.
3. Homemade Ice Cream and Crazy Cookie Bake. Hand churn ice cream and have youth bring crazy treats to decorate frosted cookies.

The Group Troupers!

Activity Ideas:

Lesson #32	**PURITY:** Self-discipline Helps Me Live a Virtuous Life *(My Future Focus Planner)*

YOU'LL NEED: Copy Future Focus Planner (page 70) and pencils for each young woman, and markers.

> Review Conclusion 2 and 3 and Teacher presentation (page 142) in Young Women Manual 1*.

ACTIVITY: Tell young women that they can focus on a positive future by making decisions about critical issues ahead of time.

> See the *"Building Integrity"* article in the New Era, *July 1999, page 15.*

This article tells us ways that we can practice integrity (e.g., *"Never let anyone persuade you to do something you know is wrong"*). Joseph is portrayed running from the temptation of Potiphar's wife. *"Joseph's personal integrity helped him make righteous choices even in difficult situations."* Because he chose to be pure ahead of time, he was able to resist the temptation when it came (Genesis 39:6-13).
1. Color My Future Focus Planner.
2. Write in the column on the right what you are willing to give up or willing to do to obtain what you want (column on the left).

COLOR SYMBOL: Color floral symbol on activity and scripture card. File activity in Young Women Value-able Journal behind value tab.

> *Choice & Accountability (orange poppy)*

PERSONAL PROGRESS* GOALS:
Beehive 1 (Individual Worth 4, Choice & Accountability 4, 5, Integrity 1, 2, 5, 6)
Beehive 2 (Choice & Accountability 2, 7, Integrity 5, 8)
Mia Maid 2 (Choice & Accountability 2, Integrity 3-4)

THOUGHT TREAT: Focus Frosted Cupcakes. Frost cupcakes, placing two gumdrops for eyes and frosting eye glass frames. Tell young women that if we set our sights high, we will be able to see past the temptations that will come. We can "look" forward to living with our Heavenly Father again, and we can "look" back on our life with pride and thanksgiving for the choices we have made.

My Future Focus Planner

What I want:	What I'm willing to give up or what I'm willing to do:
Have good friends with good values	
Have my parents trust me	
Date boys who keep Church standards	
Enjoy wholesome activities	
Marry in the temple	
Have an eternal family	

MIDWEEK ACTIVITIES:
Disciplined Demos. Ask young women to share their talents in a talent night or invite someone with a particular talent to come and tell how having discipline helped develop this talent. Tell young women that permissive or careless behavior brings loss of freedom and failure, while disciplined or correct behavior brings freedom or success. Encourage young women to develop their character by saying "no" to permissive or careless behaviors. Have young women write down (anonymously) something they struggle with (sleeping too much, telling lies, gossiping, not eating right, not exercising enough, not doing school work, not practicing music, etc.) Share an area that you need to work on, recognizing that we all have weaknesses. Place papers in a container and mix them up, then read them aloud and discuss them. Tell young women that the key to success is to let the Spirit of the Holy Ghost guide them. Challenge them to do this the rest of the week to help them cultivate disciplined behaviors. Follow up with their progress on Sunday.
HOME SHOW: Invite an architect or contractor who has built a house to speak to the young women, them take them to the house. Have the builder tell about the process of developing his or her talent and exerting the self-discipline required for this endeavor.

My Future Focus Planner

What I want:	What I'm willing to give up or what I'm willing to do:
Have good friends with good values	
Have my parents trust me	
Date boys who keep Church standards	
Enjoy wholesome activities	
Marry in the temple	
Have an eternal family	

Lesson #33	**MEDIA INFLUENCES:** I Will Avoid Degrading Media
	(TV Topper and Bookshelf Buddy)

YOU'LL NEED: Copy of TV Topper and Bookshelf Buddy quotes (page 72) for each young woman, pencils, and markers.

Review John Wesley's mother's quotation (page 144-145) and Alexander Pope's quotation (page 147) in Young Women Manual 1*.

ACTIVITY: Help young women memorize quotes and decide what they can do to choose worthy television programs, movies, books, and magazines. Write the ideas on stand-up cards. Girls can place them on their television or bookshelf to remind them to be aware of media influences.

COLOR SYMBOL: Color floral symbol on activity and scripture card. File activity in Young Women Value-able Journal behind value tab.

Choice & Accountability (orange poppy)

PERSONAL PROGRESS* GOALS:
Beehive 1 (Integrity 2)
Beehive 2 (Integrity 8)
Mia Maid 1 (Choice & Accountability 3)
Mia Maid 2 (Choice & Accountability 3, 6, Integrity 3, 5, 7)

THOUGHT TREAT: <u>TV Cookie</u>. Make a gingerbread cookie in the shape of a television. Frost and decorate with candies and a piece of licorice for the antenna. Tell young women that their life can go "down the tube" if they are not careful how they use their time and what they choose to watch on the tube (TV).

MIDWEEK ACTIVITIES: <u>Questionable Media and Questionable Cookies or Brownies</u>.

1. Prepare ahead chocolate chip cookies or brownies and have them ready on two separate plates (showing the same treat). Attach the following note to one of the plates of cookies or brownies:

Questionable Cookies
Questionable Brownies

2. With the two plates of cookies or brownies in front of girls, talk about movies, Hollywood standards, and moving ratings, etc. Lead the discussion into phrases that people use after going to these movies (for example, "The movie isn't too bad," "There's only a little swearing," "Just a little talk about sex." "You didn't see much." "I've seen worse.")

3. Tell young women you made some cookies or brownies with the best ingredients (real butter, highest grade chocolate chips). Then hold up the plate with the sign Questionable Cookies or Questionable Brownies and say, "What if I told you that in this batch I added a little bit of doggie-do? Just a little never hurt anyone. Try them. What would you do?"

4. After getting their reaction, say, "These are completely eatable cookies. There's really no doggie-do in them." Talk about ways Satan leads people "*carefully down to hell,*" by adding just a little here and there (through desensitization).

5. Read 2 Nephi 28:21. While you enjoy the cookies or brownies, make some new resolves. Have young women always ask themselves before participating in media, "Do I like doggie-do in my brownies?"

Bookshelf Buddy

What I can do to choose worthy
books and magazines:

Avoid whatever weakens your reason,
impairs the tenderness of your conscience,
obscures your sense of God,
takes off your relish for spiritual things,...
increases the authority of the body over
the mind.   —John Wesley's mother

TV Topper

What I can do to choose worthy
television programs and movies:

Vice is a
monster of so frightful mien,
As to be hated needs but to be seen;
Yet seen too oft, familiar with her face,
We first endure, then pity, then embrace.

—Alexander Pope

Lesson #34	**VIRTUE:** My Virtuous Thoughts Lead to a Virtuous Life *(Hum a Hymn hummingbird poster)*

YOU'LL NEED: Copy of bird poster (page 74) for each young woman, pencils, and markers.

Review Handout and Lesson Application (page 149) in Young Women Manual 1*.

ACTIVITY: Encourage women to select a hymn they would like to memorize. Write the words to the hymn on this poster. Read D&C 121:45. Tell young women that a hummingbird is a 3- to 6-inch bird, the smallest bird in the world. "Hummingbirds get their name from the humming sound made by their wings, which go 60 to 70 times a second" (World Book). They fly in circular fashion and collect nectar from flowers like the trumpet vine. They like to be fed sugar water. Place this water in a bird feeder by a window and watch for these hummers.

COLOR SYMBOL: Color floral symbol on activity and scripture card. File activity in Young Women Value-able Journal behind value tab.

Choice & Accountability (orange poppy)

PERSONAL PROGRESS* GOALS:
Beehive 1 (Faith 1, Knowledge 6)
Beehive 2 (Choice & Accountability 2, 5)
Mia Maid 1 (Faith 9, Knowledge 7)
Mia Maid 2 (Choice & Accountability 8)

THOUGHT TREAT: Sweet Humming. Offer sweet treats as rewards for the following. Have young women come up and hum a line or two of their favorite hymn. If a young woman guesses the hymn within 15 seconds give them a sweet treat. Give the hummer a treat for participating.

MIDWEEK ACTIVITIES:
1. Choose Your Weapon Against Immoral Thoughts. Tell young women to choose their weapon (a poem, thought, picture, song, or hymn that helps them fight immoral thoughts) and bring it with them. Have some great music, poetry, paintings that inspire, etc., ready and on

hand. Be sure to have a picture of the Savior. Talk about inspiring thoughts, pictures, songs, or hymn. Share these with each other and enjoy them. Express your love and concern for these wonderful young women and how you want them protected. Remind them of their responsibility to their future spouses and children to stay worthy and clean. Talk about pitfalls and temptations in dating that may lead to immorality.

2. Dart Weapon Throwing Contest to Fight Temptation. Write these temptations and challenges on small balloons (already blown up), then tape these onto a large poster. Talk about the fiery darts Satan sends out to tempt us (Ephesians 6:16). Divide into two teams to compete and throw darts to pop the balloon temptations. (Ahead of time tape a "FAITH" tag on each dart.) Say, "We can have our 'faith' darts ready to fight temptation."

3. Respectful Dating Panel Discussion. Select young men and women from a different stake or ward to become the panel. Young men and women can select questions on dating. Focus on how to gain respect in dating.

Hum-mmm a Hymn!

When I need to control my thoughts I'll hum a hymn!

_____
_____
_____
_____
_____
_____
_____
_____
_____
_____
_____
_____
_____
_____

"...Let virtue garnish thy
thoughts unceasingly..."
D&C 121:45

Lesson #35	RIGHTEOUSNESS: I Can Receive Blessings
	(True to the Faith Tools crossmatch journal)

YOU'LL NEED: Copy of True to the Faith Tools crossmatch journal (page 76) for each young woman, pencils, and markers.

Review Discussion and chalkboard (page 155) and Discussion (page 156) in Young Women Manual 1*.

ACTIVITY: Tell young women that they can be true to the faith in spite of worldly pressures. Follow the instructions on this crossmatch journal activity to list worldly pressures, then identify tools that will help them overcome worldly pressures and the blessings they will receive from overcoming these pressures.

COLOR SYMBOL: Color floral symbol on activity and scripture card. File activity in Young Women Value-able Journal behind value tab.

Integrity (purple pansy)

PERSONAL PROGRESS* GOALS:
Beehive 1 (Individual Worth 3, Choice & Accountability 2, Integrity 3, 4)
Beehive 2 (Choice & Accountability 3, 4, Integrity 1, 2, 4, 5, 7, 8)
Mia Maid 1 (Individual Worth 5, Choice & Accountability 8, Integrity 4)
Mia Maid 2 (Integrity 6)

THOUGHT TREAT: Blessings Cupcakes. Give each young woman a cupcake with three candles in it. Ask them to take out the candles and glue them on the Light Up My Life crossmatch (above), naming three blessings they have received. Tell them that life can be "a piece of cake" (that is, tasty and enjoyable) if they keep the commandments.

MIDWEEK ACTIVITIES:
Caterpillars. Have pictures of beautiful butterflies everywhere. Try to find a chart of how a caterpillar becomes a butterfly. Explain how it struggles for a long time to emerge from the cocoon. Tell the story of a young lady who

True to the Faith Tools

Be true to the faith in spite of worldly pressures.

List 5 worldly pressures below. Draw a line to the tool or tools that would help you overcome each worldly pressure. Then write about the blessings you would receive from overcoming each pressure.

Worldly Pressures	Blessings from Overcoming Pressures

was watching this process and decided to help. It looked like the caterpillar was having a hard time coming out of its cocoon, so she gently peeled open the cocoon a little for the butterfly. As she watched over the next few days, it came out more easily, but its body was much larger than normal and its wings were limp and frail. It could not fly but only wiggle and flop along the ground. This is because the butterfly must work hard to gain its freedom. The pressure to squeeze out of the tight cocoon pushes blood to its wings and completes the process. In the same way, pressure can make us strong. We can take the easy road or we can show discipline and courage and persistence and become much more! Make butterfly or caterpillar cookies that young women can frost and decorate to take home or make a butterfly cake (cut wings out of sheet cake). (Option: make a long caterpillar with Hostess Snowballs and licorice for the antennae.) See the New Me! Changing Caterpillar butterfly poem poster (page 96) in *Fun-tastic! Young Women Activities* (Manual 3).

True to the Faith Tools

Be true to the faith in spite of worldly pressures.

List 5 worldly pressures below. Draw a line to the tool or tools that would help you overcome each worldly pressure. Then write about the blessings you would receive from overcoming each pressure.

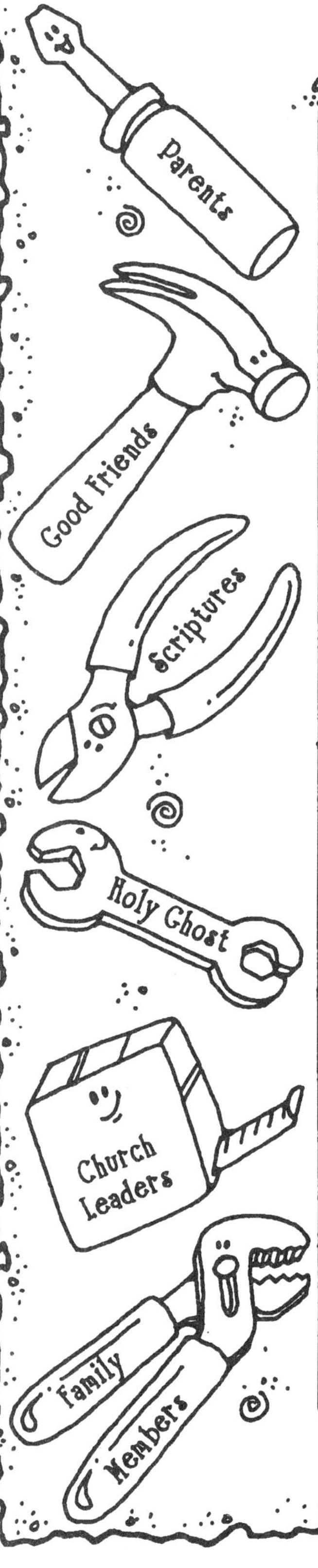

Parents

Good Friends

Scriptures

Holy Ghost

Church Leaders

Family Members

Worldly Pressures	Blessings from Overcoming Pressures

Lesson #36	**VIRTUE & TRUTH: I Seek Truth and a Virtuous Life**
	(The Keys to Virtuous Choices voting ballot)

YOU'LL NEED: Copy of Keys voting ballot (page 78) for each young woman, pencils, and markers.

Review Scriptures (Moroni 7:15-17) on page 160 in Young Women Manual 1*.

ACTIVITY: Tell young women that Heavenly Father has given us the keys to determine good from evil.
1. Read Moroni 7:15-17.
2. Have young women read choices on voting ballot and vote "good" or "bad" by checking the box. They can use the following keys to determine their answer: "Does it invite me to do good? Will it strengthen my faith in Christ?"

COLOR SYMBOL: Color floral symbol on activity and scripture card. File activity in Young Women Value-able Journal behind value tab.

Choice & Accountability (orange poppy)

PERSONAL PROGRESS* GOALS:
Beehive 1 (Choice & Accountability 4, 5, 6, 7, Integrity 3)
Beehive 2 (Choice & Accountability 2, 5, Integrity 1, 5)
Mia Maid 1 (Integrity 2)
Mia Maid 2 (Choice & Accountability 3, Integrity 1)

THOUGHT TREAT: Video Tape No-bologna Sandwich. Make a bologna sandwich for each young woman, cutting off the top third and crust (to make a small rectangle). Remove the top slice of bread and cut two holes in it, using a 1-inch lid (so sandwich looks like a video tape). Place top back on sandwich. Wrap in clear wrap. Tell young women that this Video Tape No-bologna Sandwich is to remind us that eternal life is real (no-bologna). Everything we do is video taped to view eternally. We can make our life's movie one to be proud of by choosing virtuous actions.

MIDWEEK ACTIVITIES:
Guest Daters Dating Panel Discussion. Invite young men of dating age from another ward or stake to come and talk about dating. Ask them to talk about moral dating choices and how young people can avoid intimate situations. Have young women prepare questions in advance.
SAMPLE QUESTIONS: What do you look for when you ask a girl out for a date? How can you tell if a girl has high standards? How do you like a girl to act on a date? What should or shouldn't a girl wear on a date? How does a girl say no to a kiss? How can a girl say no to physical advances? If a girl likes you but doesn't want to kiss on the date, how can she keep your mind off the kiss? How can a girl show you she likes you without kissing? What does a girl need to do to earn your respect? Do you like a girl to ask you out? If so, how should she ask you out without seeming aggressive? Do you like girls to flirt with you? How can she flirt with you without appearing too bold? What kinds of activities make dating fun? What date activities help you to get to know a girl better? How do you rate a girl? What do you look for? How should a girl show interest in you?

Keys to Virtuous Choices

Will it strengthen my faith in Christ?

Does it invite me to do good?

Moroni 7:15-17

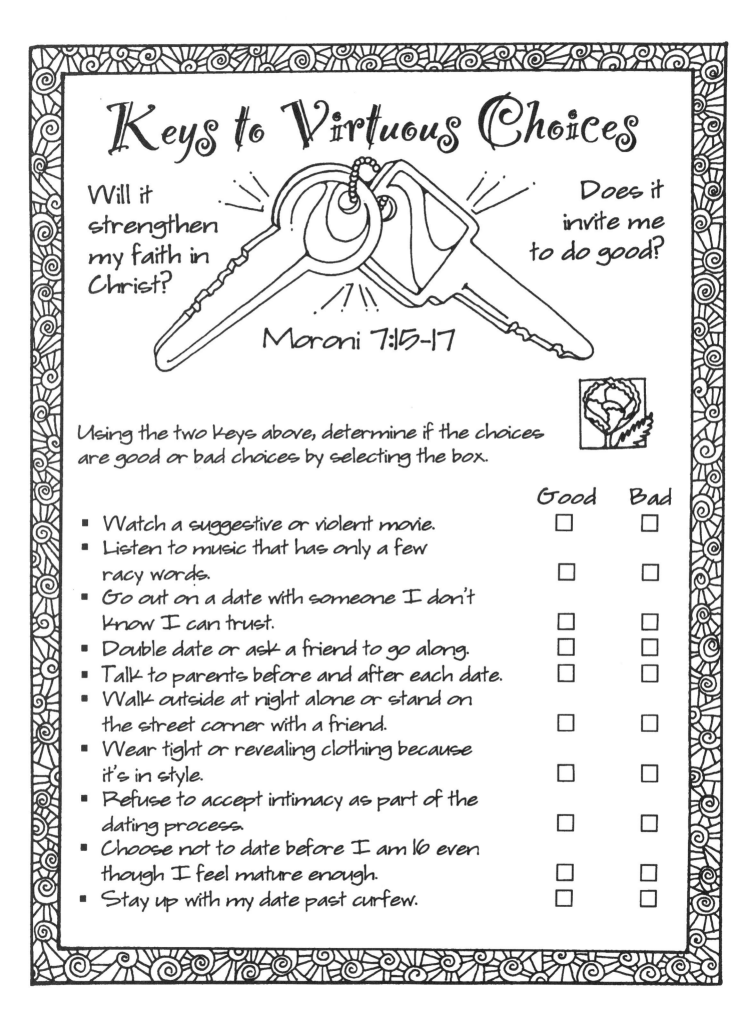

Using the two keys above, determine if the choices are good or bad choices by selecting the box.

	Good	Bad
Watch a suggestive or violent movie.	☐	☐
Listen to music that has only a few racy words.	☐	☐
Go out on a date with someone I don't know I can trust.	☐	☐
Double date or ask a friend to go along.	☐	☐
Talk to parents before and after each date.	☐	☐
Walk outside at night alone or stand on the street corner with a friend.	☐	☐
Wear tight or revealing clothing because it's in style.	☐	☐
Refuse to accept intimacy as part of the dating process.	☐	☐
Choose not to date before I am 16 even though I feel mature enough.	☐	☐
Stay up with my date past curfew.	☐	☐

Lesson #37	**SELF-CARE: I Will Keep My Body and Mind in Condition** *(I'm a Living Doll design-a-doll goal chart)*

YOU'LL NEED: Copy of doll front and back (pages 80-81) and string or yarn for each young woman, yarn the color of each girl's hair, fabric scraps, scissors, glue, and markers.

> *Review Preparation #3 and #4 (page 164) in Young Women Manual 1*.*

ACTIVITY: Help each young woman to see herself as "a living doll" and increase her desire to take care of her mind and body.
1. Color and cut out head and body.
2. Have young women draw in their own face.
3. Glue yarn on for hair and fabric for clothes.
4. On the back write goals, looking up scriptures for inspiration.
5. Glue a string down the center and glue the images back to back. Make sure the top has 3-4 inches at the top to hang image in their room.

COLOR SYMBOL: Color floral symbol on activity and scripture card. File activity in Young Women Value-able Journal behind value tab.

> *Individual Worth (red rose)*

PERSONAL PROGRESS* GOALS:
Beehive 1 (Knowledge 4)
Beehive 2 (Individual Worth 3, 4,
Knowledge 1, 5, 6, Choice & Accountability 2)

THOUGHT TREAT: Living Doll Gingerbread Girls. Make gingerbread dough and cut in the shapes of gingerbread girls. Decorate to look like individual young women to personalize each cookie.

MIDWEEK ACTIVITIES:
1. Healthy Heart and Change of Heart.
Step #1. Take young women to a track or other place to run or walk. Explain that this is not a race; they can run or walk. Take their pulse and have them run/walk around the track. Take their pulse again. Talk about exercise and how it strengthens the heart.
Step #2. Ask them to write about a conflict with their parents or a family member (what the young women did, what the other person did). Put the paper in a sealed envelope with their name on it.
Step #3. As they go around the track again, have them think how they could have handled things differently.
Step #4. Have young women write their change of heart on the envelope. Talk about a healthy heart (physically), a change of heart (spiritually) and striving to be more self-reliant through better control of our responses to conflict. An understanding heart is a helping heart.
Step #5. Finish with a light-hearted activity: Go out after for smoothies and play games.
2. Fitness Pro Question and Answer Night.
Have a fitness professional come and show young women some basic things they can do to stay active, and to discuss how to gain physical strength through exercises, weights, and walking. Play volleyball or basketball, do exercises, or dance. Serve a blender drink (with protein powder), or have fruit and yogurt available, allowing girls to place yogurt in a bowl, add, and blend their own choice of fruit.

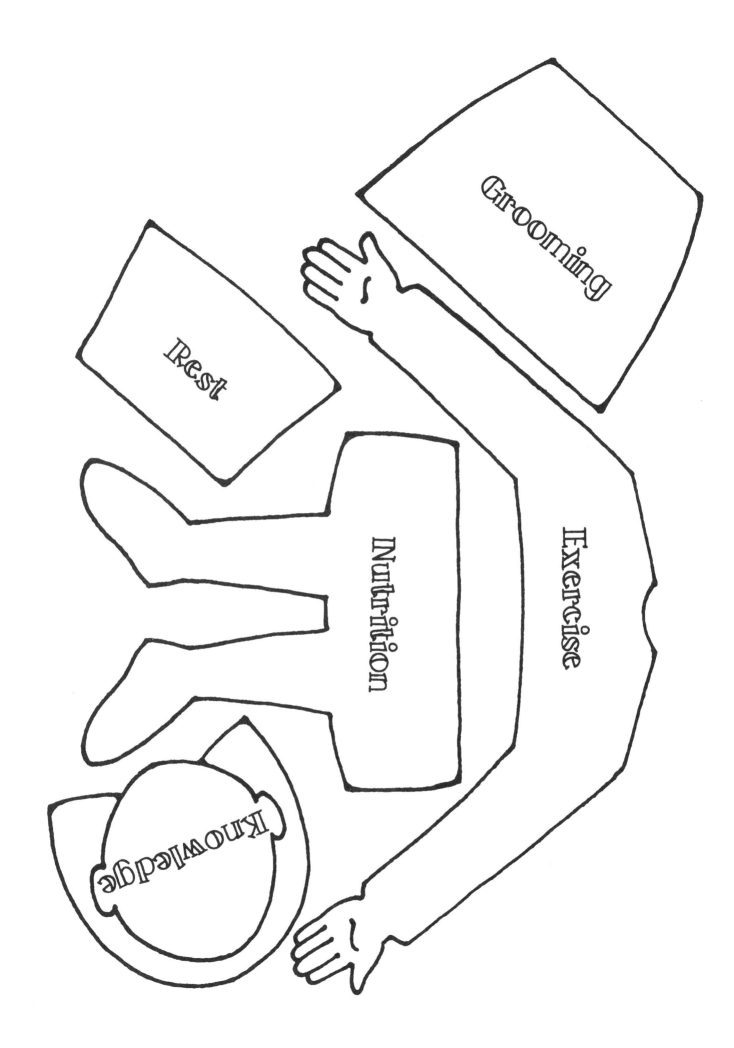

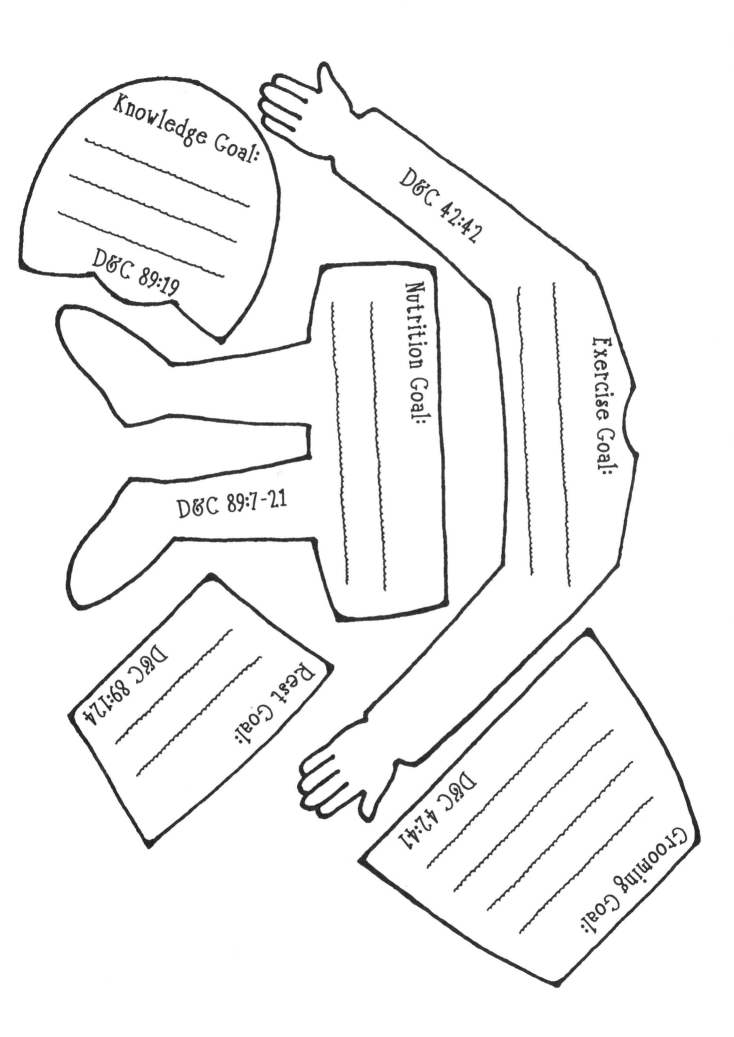

Knowledge Goal:

D&C 89:19

D&C 42:42

Nutrition Goal:

Exercise Goal:

D&C 89:7-21

Rest Goal:

D&C 89:124

Grooming Goal:

D&C 42:41

Lesson #38	**WORD OF WISDOM:** I Will Practice Good Nutrition
	(healthful food refrigerator magnets)

YOU'LL NEED: Copy of refrigerator magnets (page 83) and 5 (½" magnets with glue on back) for each young woman, scissors, and markers.

ACTIVITY: Tell young women that good nutrition is part of keeping the Word of Wisdom. If we can concentrate on high-nutrition rather than low-nutrition foods, we will be blessed, as it says in D&C 89:18-21. Make these refrigerator magnets to use as reminders. (1) Color and cut out healthy food images. Laminate if possible. (2) Glue a magnet on the back of each to stick on the refrigerator.

COLOR SYMBOL: Color floral symbol on activity and scripture card. File activity in Young Women Value-able Journal behind value tab.

Individual Worth (red rose)

PERSONAL PROGRESS* GOALS:
Beehive 1 (Divine Nature 1),
Beehive 2 (Divine Nature 8, Good Works 7, Integrity 7),
Mia Maid 1 (Individual Worth 4, 9, Integrity 6)

THOUGHT TREAT #1: High-Nutrition Foods and a Low-Nutrition Food. Offer two (low-calorie) high-nutrition foods, e.g., celery and an apple, and one (high-calorie) low-nutrition item, e.g, cupcake. Compare the difference in nutrients and the difference in the energy provided by each.

THOUGHT TREAT #2: Serve some seeds, corn, grains, nuts, fruit, vegetables, whole grain muffins, or cornbread with honey. Have a discussion about the benefits of each.

MIDWEEK ACTIVITIES:
1. Plant Some Nutritional Ideas. Show real plants or drawings of (1) a plant that has had little water, little sunlight, and no fertilizer, and (2) a plant that is healthy due to water, sunlight, fertilizer, etc. Explain that we are made of the same molecules, and our body requires certain nutrients to retain health. Some foods are poison to our bodies and some foods are medicine to our bodies. You can see people who are not caring for themselves properly and those who are. Some people look tired and pale.

Others look bright and energetic! Talk about the story of Daniel as a youth in the king's court (Daniel 1:8-16). Explain that verse 12 *"pulse to eat"* means foods made of seeds, grains, etc.; see also Mosiah 9:8-9; D&C 89:14. Talk about the role of protein, carbohydrates, and fats. Note that the body needs balance.

2. Vitamin Visit to the Library. Take young women to the library to look at diet, nutrition, cookbooks, etc., in the adult and the children's sections of the library. Have them photocopy a short piece to share with the others. Have each young woman share her discoveries about healthful, vitamin-rich foods and how they will help their body. Encourage young women to copy at least one healthful recipe they wish to prepare for their family.

3. Healthful Food Tasting Table. Have young women bring a healthful dish to sample along with copies of recipes. Be sure they sign their name on the recipe.

4. Snack Attack Cures. Have young women share ideas for their favorite healthful snacks. Have them tell why this snack is good for them, e.g., an apple is 85% water and high in fiber ("nature's scrub brush"), celery calms the nerves and is also high in fiber.

5. Health Food Store Tour. Call ahead to have someone from a health food store give young women a tour and a sample of carrot or green juice. Learn about soy products, sprouted bread, tofu/soy cheese, cream cheese and sour cream, healthy hot dogs, peanut butter without sugar, nuts, seeds, whole grains, soy margarine, wheat meat, protein powder, whole grain cereals, wheat grass, healing herbs, vitamins, essential oils, and more. Young women can also look at books, magazines, and cosmetics.

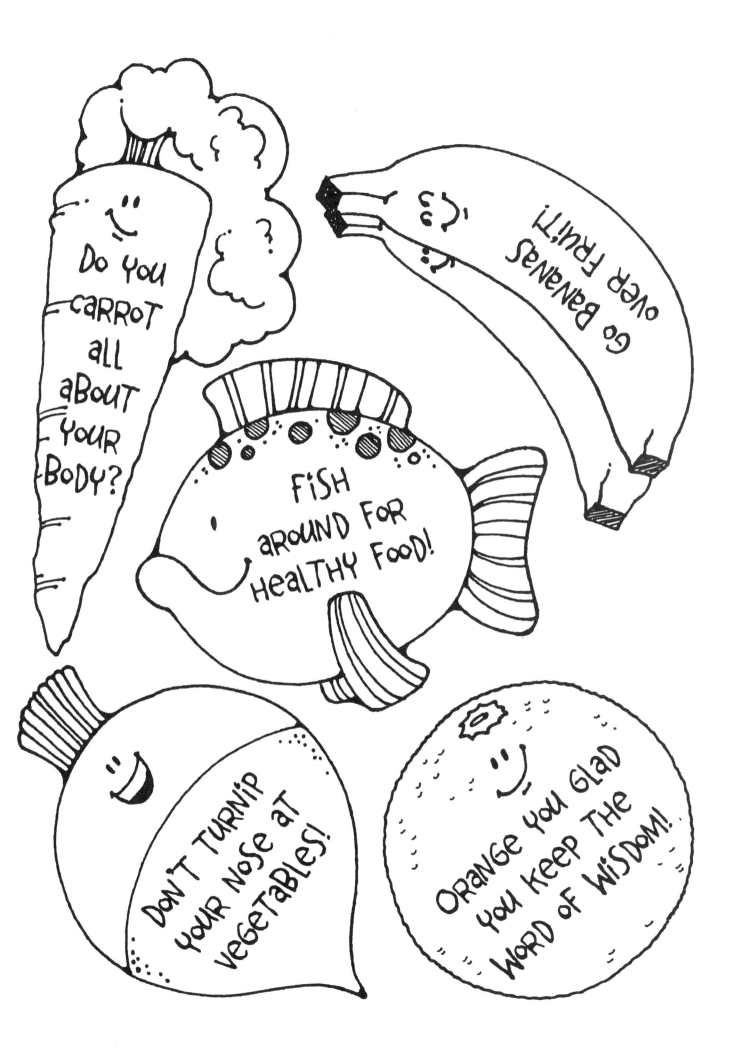

Lesson #39	**DRUG ABUSE Affects My Body and Spirit** *(Drug Free Me word find puzzle)*

YOU'LL NEED: Copy of word find puzzle (page 85) for each young woman, pencils, and markers.

Review Chalkboard discussion #1-5 and Optional class member presentation #1-5 (pages 172-173) in Young Women Manual 1*.

ACTIVITY: Follow the puzzle instructions and write ways you plan to resist and not give into taking drugs.

<u>Drugs Found on Puzzles</u>: marijuana, tobacco, caffeine, LSD, cocaine, crack, alcohol, heroin, barbiturates, amphetamines, diet pills.

<u>Reasons for Drug Involvement</u>: peer pressure, escape, immaturity, availability, advertising appeal.

COLOR SYMBOL: Color floral symbol on activity and scripture card. File activity in Young Women Value-able Journal behind value tab.

Individual Worth (red rose)

PERSONAL PROGRESS* GOALS:
<u>Beehive 1</u> (Faith 6)
<u>Mia Maid 2</u> (Choice & Accountability 4)

THOUGHT TREAT: <u>Orange Juice</u>. Serve young women orange juice as you tell these or other stories where someone has resisted alcohol or drugs.

STORY #1: A 22-year-old-Latter-day Saint woman went to a large city where she taught in a modeling agency. Before the agency convention they were all drinking alcohol except the LDS girl, who asked for orange juice. She was unaware that others were watching until a half hour after the convention started. The director asked her to stand in front of the 60 guests to announce that she was the only teetotaler (nondrinker) in the group. She sat down with a stronger conviction to keep her ideals.

STORY #2: This same young woman at age 21

invited many college students to her home. With her parents' help, they enjoyed games, food, and dancing. She went out onto the patio to check on her guests to find three young men drinking beer by themselves. She simply said, "We have a lot of fun at our parties. We don't drink beer at our parties, so why don't you come in and find out." They stashed the beer away and said later that they had a great time!

MIDWEEK ACTIVITIES:
<u>**Drugs Question and Answer Session.**</u> Have a qualified police officer, e.g., from the DARE Program, come in and talk to young women about drugs. Have a question and answer brainstorm before the officer comes, with one or two young women presenting these questions. Encourage young women to ask questions there. Bake a plate of yummy but healthful treats for the officer with a note of appreciation signed by the girls. Quick Treat Ideas: Make a poster warning against drugs, using candy bars, e.g., Create "Joy" - Keep Off Drugs (Almond Joy bar). If young men are invited, give them a Big Hunk candy bar and say "Be a Big Hunk and say 'no' to drugs."

Drug Free Me!

Blackout the squares with the X's and then cross out the drugs you find in the puzzle. Some may appear backwards in the puzzle. Then find 5 reasons why some young people become involved with drugs (words also may be backwards). Fill in the blanks with the words and write next to them ways you plan to overcome and not give into taking drugs.

O	C	C	A	B	O	T	P	E	E	R	H	E	R	O	I	N
X	X	C	R	A	C	K	S	L	L	I	P	T	E	I	D	E
D	S	L	X	X	X	X	E	R	U	S	S	E	R	P	X	N
C	R	A	N	K	G	N	I	S	I	T	R	E	V	D	A	I
X	Y	T	I	R	U	T	A	M	M	I	D	E	E	P	S	A
L	A	E	P	P	A	X	M	A	R	I	J	U	A	N	A	C
X	Y	T	I	L	I	B	A	L	I	A	V	A	X	X	X	O
A	M	P	H	E	T	A	M	I	N	E	S	X	X	X	X	C
X	L	O	H	O	C	L	A	X	E	S	C	A	P	E	X	X

1. P_____
   P_____

2. E_____

3. I_____

4. A_____

5. A_____
   A_____

Lesson #40	**HEALTH CARE:** I Will Provide Basic Health Care Skills in My Home
	(Baby-sitter's Information Sheet)

YOU'LL NEED: Several copies of Baby-sitter's Information Sheet (page 87) for each young woman, scissors, and markers.

> *Review Teacher presentation #3 (page 179) in Young Women Manual 1*.*

ACTIVITY: Give young women several copies of the Baby-sitter's Information Sheet to take with them when they babysit. This will help them obtain the correct information so they will be better prepared with emergency telephone numbers, e.g., police or fire department, poison control, and family doctor without having to take time to look up the numbers in the phone book. Young women can post the information by the phone and feel more confident in their child care responsibilities. Parents will also be more at ease having this vital information at their fingertips.

COLOR SYMBOL: Color floral symbol on activity and scripture card. File activity in Young Women Value-able Journal behind value tab.

Knowledge (green ivy)

PROGRESS* GOALS:
Beehive 1 (Good Works 4)
Beehive 2 (Knowledge 1, 5, 6)

THOUGHT TREAT: Red Cross Licorice.
1. Cut two 6-inch pieces of licorice to tie together to make a red cross.
2. Tell young women that the American Red Cross has millions of volunteers in hospitals and community agencies giving money, blood, training, and first aid to disaster victims in an emergency.
3. Obtain several books from the library or American Red Cross to show Young Women.
4. Demonstrate a skill or two, giving them the licorice after they have tried the skill.

MIDWEEK ACTIVITIES:
American Red Cross ✚ Nurse Notes
Have young women stand by with a notepad for these activities.
✚ Put a girl in bed. Have a nurse show how to care for her.
✚ Go visit someone in your area who is ill and in bed. Make arrangements ahead of time for this visit so the nurse can tell how she/he cares for the patient. Have a tour of the nurses station and supply closet (if allowed).
✚ Do book reviews on the American Red Cross or other first-aid book.
✚ Have a paramedic come and show emergency health care, CPR, etc.
✚ Visit a daycare and talk about how you would save that child's life or limb if needed.
✚ Talk about the emergency items you need in a first-aid kit and how to use these items.
✚ Have a nurse tell you the latest items for first-aid kits.
✚ Have a CERT (Community Emergency Response Team) active volunteer or a member from your local fire department share ideas.
✚ Show a film on first-aid skills.

Baby-sitters Information Sheet

Family Names and Address:

Parents' Names _____

Children's Names _____

Home Address _____

Parents will be at:

Place _____

Address _____

Phone No. _____ Time Returning _____

Nearby Friend or Relative:

Name _____ Phone No. _____

Emergency Information:

◊ Police or Fire Department: _____

◊ Poison Control: _____

◊ Family Doctor: _____
Name _____ Phone No. _____

Baby-sitters Information Sheet

Family Names and Address:

Parents' Names _____

Children's Names _____

Home Address _____

Parents will be at:

Place _____

Address _____

Phone No. _____ Time Returning _____

Nearby Friend or Relative:

Name _____ Phone No. _____

Emergency Information:

◊ Police or Fire Department: _____

◊ Poison Control: _____

◊ Family Doctor: _____
Name _____ Phone No. _____

Lesson #41	**SUCCESS: I Recognize My Ability to Succeed**
	(My Success Garden goal plan)

YOU'LL NEED: Copy of Success Garden goal plan (page 89) for each young woman, pencils, and markers.

Review Activity (page 182) in Young Women Manual 1*.

ACTIVITY: Encourage young women to plant in their garden of life things that are of great worth and value (testimony, education, love for family and friends). Remind them they must—
Step #1. Weed their garden. Read 2 Nephi 8:3 and write things they want to change.
Step #2. Plant their garden. Read D&C 59:17-18 and write talents they want to develop.
Step #3. Water and nurture their garden. Read Isaiah 58:11 and decide how they will use their time and energy to create a successful garden. (See Thought Treat below for more ideas.)

COLOR SYMBOL: Color floral symbol on activity and scripture card. File activity in Young Women Value-able Journal behind value tab.

Choice & Accountability (orange poppy)

PERSONAL PROGRESS* GOALS:
Beehive 1 (Knowledge 4)
Beehive 2 (Individual Worth 3, 4, Integrity 2)
Mia Maid 2 (Divine Nature 6)

THOUGHT TREAT: Fresh Garden Snacks. Tell young women, "Imagine what your garden would be like if you didn't weed, plant, water, and nurture it. Think about your life's garden and what it would be like if you didn't take care of it. Now, imagine life without success and also with it. Look for the success in each day and remember that success is a journey. So 'plot' your garden plan and nourish your garden."

MIDWEEK ACTIVITIES:
1. Attitude Adjustment. In this "put-down" world, do a "face-lift" activity. Have some moms come and pamper their daughters. If you can get

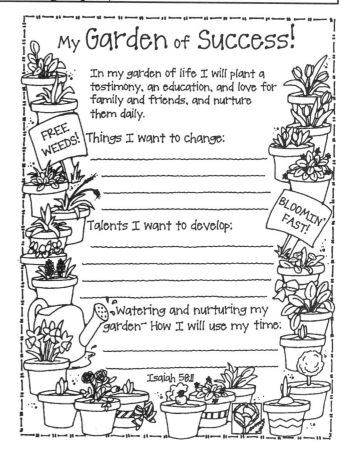

My Garden of Success!

In my garden of life I will plant a testimony, an education, and love for family and friends, and nurture them daily.

FREE WEEDS!

Things I want to change:
_____
_____
_____

Talents I want to develop:
_____
_____
_____

BLOOMIN' FAST!

"Watering and nurturing my garden" How I will use my time:
_____
_____

Isaiah 58:11

someone with a salon great; but if not, just make do with what you have. Have moms wash their daughters' hair, do their nails, give a facial, neck massage, etc. Have each mother write a letter to their daughter ahead of time, expressing her belief in her, that she can make it through this world of ups and downs. Then have a slim treat!
2. Success Seminar. Have different speakers who are experts in one skill or another train young women to live in this world of competition, and live with honor. Have them talk about treating others with respect as girls pursue their education and career both inside and outside the home. Talk about how to organize and make the best use of their time. Have speakers tell how they use success tools such as a planner, phone, computer, and office equipment to succeed. Some could talk about successful home careers and the advantages of working at home. They could also talk about the skills they would need to work at home.

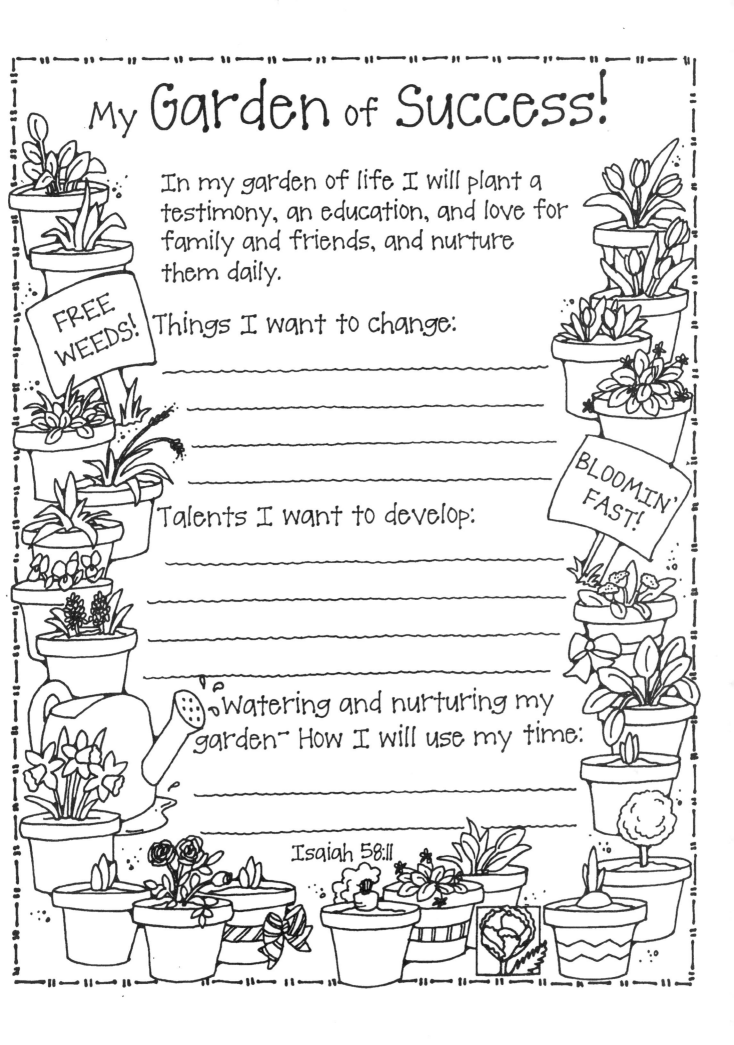

My Garden of Success!

In my garden of life I will plant a testimony, an education, and love for family and friends, and nurture them daily.

FREE WEEDS!

Things I want to change:

_____

_____

_____

_____

Talents I want to develop:

_____

_____

_____

BLOOMIN' FAST!

_____

Watering and nurturing my garden~ How I will use my time:

_____

_____

Isaiah 58:11

| *Lesson #42* | **SELF-IMPROVEMENT:** I Will Accept Opportunities to Improve
(mirror motivators) |

Take the plunge! I must dive in and do it. I'm only wasting time if I sit on the shore.

Confidence is a gift I can give myself. If I wait for others to give me the confidence I need, I may never succeed!

Practice releases pressure! Each time I try to do something difficult, it becomes easier the next time.

YOU'LL NEED: Copy of motivators (page 91) for each young woman, scissors, and markers.

Review Activity (page 187) in Young Women Manual 1*.

ACTIVITY: Give each young woman a set of mirror motivators. Tell them that we will have many opportunities in life to improve ourselves. If we take advantage of them we will grow into the woman Heavenly Father wants us to be, especially when we pray for the strength to try. Post these messages on your mirror to motivate.
1. Color and cut out motivators.
2. Write goals on the back of each motivator that fit the motivational message on the front. Goals could be written with backward letters so young women can read them in the mirror.
3. Post messages on the mirror.

COLOR SYMBOL: Color floral symbol on activity and scripture card. File activity in Young Women Value-able Journal behind value tab.

Individual Worth (red rose)

PERSONAL PROGRESS* GOALS:
<u>Beehive 1</u> (Integrity 1, Individual Worth 8)
<u>Beehive 2</u> (Knowledge 5, 6, Choice &
Accountability 8, Integrity 2)
<u>Mia Maid 1</u> (Choice & Accountability 2)

THOUGHT TREAT: <u>YOU Designer Bread.</u>
Shape three 4-inch balls of raised bread dough into the Y, O, and U shapes. Bake 15-20 minutes at 350 degrees and then butter. Put the bread letter shapes in a basket and ask young women to find the letters YOU and eat them. Talk about your future opportunities that YOU have and what YOU will do to prepare for them.

MIDWEEK ACTIVITIES:
1. <u>Fight Fear Brainstorm.</u> Have signs around the room that say "phone fears," "scary things," "talking traps," "saying no," "nightmares," "stranger danger," "babysitting fears," etc. Have each young woman write one of her fears on a slip of paper, e.g., talking

to strangers, asking for directions, etc. (without giving her name). Put the papers in a hat, then draw and discuss them one at a time. Young women might even role-play a scary situation and how best to react. This may give some ideas and encouragement to help them overcome these fears so they can face any future challenges with greater awareness.
2. <u>Balloon Beauty Shop.</u> Blow up a helium balloon for each young woman. Have young women draw their face and favorite hairstyle on the balloon and write their name. Tie it to the back of their chair or arm. If leaders design these balloon heads ahead of time, tie balloons to a chair and ask young women to find their balloon and sit in that chair. Set up chairs in a circle or semi-circle. The leader or special guest can share beauty tips and tricks and ask young women to participate and share their ideas. Some young women can volunteer to have their hair designed to show hair accessories.
3. <u>Self-improvement Search.</u> Take young women to the library to search through books that will give them a desire to improve (e.g., beauty, self-esteem, health, motivation). Reserve a conference room or check out the books and go out on the lawn or back to the church to share ideas.

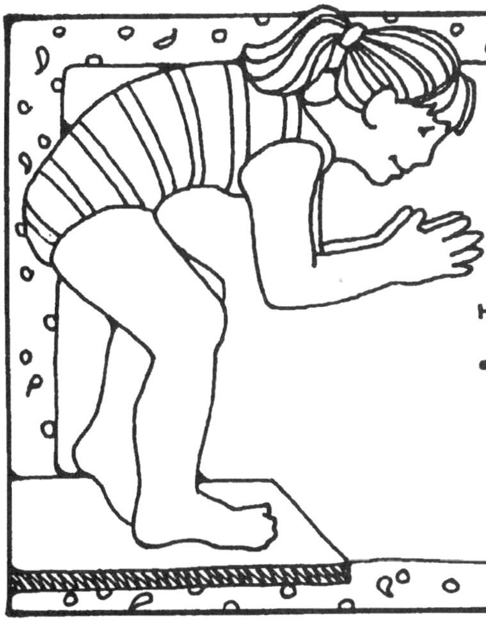

Take the plunge!
I must dive in and do it.
I'm only wasting time if I
sit on the shore.

Confidence is a gift I
can give myself. If I
wait for others to give
me the confidence I
need, I may never succeed!

Practice releases pressure!
Each time I try to do
something difficult, it becomes
easier the next time.

Lesson #43	**RIGHTEOUSNESS: My Self-esteem Comes from Righteous Living**
	(I'm Sailing! Keep Spiritual Boat Afloat game)

YOU'LL NEED: Copy of *I'm Sailing!* game board and scripture cards (pages 93-95), with game rules (below), and a small envelope for each young woman, scissors, markers, and dice.

Review Lesson Application (page 191) in Young Women Manual 1.

ACTIVITY: With this game young women search the scriptures to find ways they can gain self-esteem through righteous living.
1. Color and cut out game board, scripture cards, and game rules (below).
2. Place game pieces in an envelope and tape to the back of the game board.

I'm Sailing!
I Will Keep My Spiritual Boat Afloat!
GAME RULES: This game will help players sail through troubled waters by living the gospel of Jesus Christ.
1. Provide a copy of the standard works for each guest or have one set of scriptures for every two players.
2. Turn SUNKEN SHIP, LIFESAVER, and ANCHOR scripture cards face up in separate piles on the table or floor.
3. Divide into two teams with a boat marker for each team at the START position.
4. Teams take turns rolling a dice and moving 1-6 spaces on the board.
5. When player lands on a SUNKEN SHIP, LIFESAVER, or ANCHOR, she draws a matching scripture card. Player reads the scripture aloud and identifies a key word or words that tell us how to keep our spiritual boat afloat (and avoid sinking). If players agree on the key word, that team earns 10 points.
6. When player lands on CALM SEA or RAPID WAVES, both teams can rush to find a scripture that describes a CALM SEA (righteousness) or RAPID WAVES (wickedness). The first team to find their scripture earns 30 points and one of their players reads the scripture aloud.
7. Players keep moving around the board until the first team earns 100 or 200 points.

COLOR SYMBOL: Color floral symbol on activity and scripture card. File activity in Young Women Value-able Journal behind value tab.

Integrity (purple pansy)

PERSONAL PROGRESS* GOALS:
Beehive 2 (Choice & Accountability 8, Integrity 1, 3)
Beehive 2 (Integrity 4, 5, 7, 8)
Mia Maid 1 (Divine Nature 5, Integrity 4-6)
Mia Maid 2 (Choice & Accountability 5, Integrity 3, 6)

THOUGHT TREAT: Twinkie Boat. Give each young woman a Hostess Twinkie or Tiger Tail (coconut with a raspberry stripe) found at the Hostess Bakery or grocery store. Copy the following note below and cut into a sail shape. Tape it to a toothpick and insert the "sail" into the Twinkie.

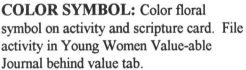

To keep my spiritual boat afloat, I will read the scriptures daily, pray for guidance, and serve with a willing heart.

MIDWEEK ACTIVITY:
Ego Boosters Brainstorm. Discuss how you feel when you feel welcome and loved and how you feel when others care for you. Give each young woman a pen and pencil to write ways they can boost others' ego, build them up, fellowship them, and make them feel good. Young women can share their ideas of how others have done this for them and discuss things they would like to do in the future.

 *Young Women Manual 1 and Personal Progress books are published by The Church of Jesus Christ of Latter-day Saints, Salt Lake City, Utah.

SUNKEN SHIP: *"It is by the prayers of the righteous that ye are spared."* - Alma 10:23	**SUNKEN SHIP:** *"Jesus answered and said unto them, Ye do err, not knowing the scriptures, nor the power of God."* - Matthew 22:29
ANCHOR: *"Pray always, lest you enter into temptation and lose your reward."* - D&C 31:12	
SUNKEN SHIP: *"It is for the righteous' sake that [the city] is spared. But behold, the time cometh, saith the Lord, that when ye shall cast out the righteous from among you, then shall ye be ripe for destruction."* - Helaman 13:14	**LIFESAVER:** *(speaking of Jesus Christ) "Neither is there salvation in any other: for there is none other name under heaven given among men, whereby we must be saved."* - Acts 4:12
SUNKEN SHIP: *"He [Satan] flattereth them, and leadeth them along until he draggeth their souls down to hell; and thus he causeth them to catch themselves in their own snare. And thus he goeth up and down, to and fro in the earth, seeking to destroy the souls of men."* - D&C 10:26-27	**LIFESAVER:** *"Because ye are compelled to be humble blessed are ye; for a man sometimes, if he is compelled to be humble, seeketh repentance; and now surely, whosoever repenteth shall find mercy; and he that findeth mercy and endureth to the end the same shall be saved."* - Alma 32:13
ANCHOR: *"We believe in Christ, we keep the law of Moses, and look forward with steadfastness into Christ, until the law shall be fulfilled."* - 2 Nephi 25:24	**LIFESAVER:** *"We are made alive in Christ because of our faith; yet we keep the law because of the commandments. And we talk of Christ, we preach of Christ, we prophesy of Christ, and we write according to our prophecies, that our children may know to what source they may look for remission of their sins."* - 2 Nephi 25:25-26
SUNKEN SHIP: *"But the wicked are like the troubled sea, when it cannot rest, whose waters cast up mire and dirt. There is no peace, saith my God to the wicked."* - Isaiah 57:20-21	
LIFESAVER: *"Because of the righteousness of [the Lord's] people, Satan has no power ... over the hearts of the people, for they dwell in righteousness, and the Holy one of Israel reigneth."* - 1 Nephi 22:26	**ANCHOR:** *"He that repenteth and exerciseth faith, and bringeth forth good works, and prayeth continually without ceasing—unto such it is given to know the mysteries of God."* - Alma 26:22
SUNKEN SHIP: *"Yea, wo be unto him that hearkeneth unto the precepts of men, and denieth the power of God and the gift of the Holy Ghost."* - 2 Nephi 28:26	**LIFESAVER:** *"And if thou draw out thy soul to the hungry, and satisfy the afflicted soul; then shall thy light rise in obscurity, and thy darkness be as the noonday."* - Isaiah 58:10
ANCHOR: *"The commandments of God must be fulfilled. And if it so be that the children of men keep the commandments of God he doth nourish them, and strengthen them, and provide means whereby they can accomplish the thing which he has commanded them; wherefore he did provide means for us while we did sojourn in the wilderness."* - 1 Nephi 17:3	**LIFESAVER:** *"If ye by the grace of God are perfect in Christ, and deny not his power, then are ye sanctified in Christ by the grace of God, through the shedding of the blood of Christ, which is in the covenant of the Father unto remission of your sins, that ye become holy, without spot."* - Moroni 10:33
SUNKEN SHIP: *"Remember the awfulness in transgressing against that Holy God, and also the awfulness of yielding to the enticings of that cunning one. Remember, to be carnally-minded is death, and to be spiritually-minded is life eternal."* - 2 Nephi 9:39	**LIFESAVER:** *"Turn to the Lord with all your mind, might, and strength; that ye lead away the hearts of no more to do wickedly; but rather return unto them, and acknowledge your faults and that wrong which ye have done."* - Alma 39:13
LIFESAVER: *"The righteous ... shall inherit the kingdom of God, which was prepared for them from the foundation of the world, and their joy shall be full forever."* - 2 Nephi 9:18	**LIFESAVER:** *"The righteous that hearken unto the words of the prophets, and destroy them not, but look forward unto Christ with steadfastness for the signs which are given, notwithstanding all persecution—behold, they are they which shall not perish."* - 2 Nephi 26:8
SUNKEN SHIP: *"... If ye should transgress and go contrary to that which has been spoken, that ye do withdraw yourselves from the Spirit of the Lord, that it may have no place in you to guide you in wisdom's path that ye may be blessed, prospered, and preserved..."* - Mosiah 2:36	**SUNKEN SHIP:** *"The man ... that cometh out in open rebellion against God; therefore he listeth to obey the evil spirit, and becometh an enemy to all righteousness; therefore, the Lord has no place in him, for he dwelleth not in unholy temples."* - Mosiah 2:37

SUNKEN SHIP: *"Except ye repent, ye shall all likewise perish."* - Luke 13:3	**LIFESAVER:** *"Pray always, and I will pour out my Spirit upon you, and great shall be your blessing."* - D&C 19:38
SUNKEN SHIP: *"I will judge you, O house of Israel, every one according to his ways, saith the Lord God. Repent, and turn yourselves from all your transgressions; so iniquity shall not be your ruin."* - Ezekiel 18:30	**ANCHOR:** *"All nations, kindreds, tongues, and people shall dwell safely in the Holy One of Israel if it so be that they will repent."* - 1 Nephi 22:28
ANCHOR: *"Whosoever repenteth , and hardeneth not his heart, he shall have claim on mercy through mine only Begotten Son, unto a remission of his sins; and these shall enter into my rest."* - Alma 12:34	**LIFESAVER:** *"Now Aaron began to open the scriptures unto them concerning the coming of Christ, and also concerning the resurrection of the dead, and that there could be no redemption for mankind save it were through the death and sufferings of Christ, and the atonement of his blood."* - Alma 21:9
LIFESAVER: *"O remember, remember, my sons, the words which king Benjamin spake unto his people; yea, remember that there is no other way nor means whereby man can be saved, only through the atoning blood of Jesus Christ, who shall come; yea, remember that he cometh to redeem the world."* - Helaman 5:9	**SUNKEN SHIP:** *"Can ye imagine yourselves brought before the tribunal of God with your souls filled with guilt and remorse, having a remembrance of all your guilt, yea, a perfect remembrance of all your wickedness, yea, a remembrance that ye have set at defiance the commandments of God?"* - Alma 5:18
LIFESAVER: *"Ye should consider on the blessed and happy state of those that keep the commandments of God. For behold, they are blessed in all things, both temporal and spiritual; and if they hold out faithful to the end they are received into heaven, that thereby they may dwell with God in a state of never-ending happiness. O remember, remember that these things are true; for the Lord God hath spoken it."* - Mosiah 2:41	**ANCHOR:** *"It is upon the rock of our Redeemer, who is Christ, the Son of God, that ye must build your foundation; that when the devil shall send forth his mighty winds, yea, his shafts in the whirlwind, yea, when all his hail and his mighty storm shall beat upon you, it shall have no power over you to drag you down to the gulf of misery and endless wo, because of the rock upon which ye are built, which is a sure foundation, a foundation whereon if men build they cannot fail."* - Helaman 5:12
SUNKEN SHIP: *"And the Lord will set his hand again the second time to restore his people from their lost and fallen state. Wherefore, he will proceed to do a marvelous work and a wonder among the children of men."* - 2 Nephi 25:17	**SUNKEN SHIP:** *"I command you again to repent, lest I humble you with my almighty power; and that you confess your sins, lest you suffer these punishments of which I have spoken, of which in the smallest, yea, even in the least degree you have tasted at the time I withdrew my Spirit."* - D&C 19:20
LIFESAVER: *"Wherefore, ye must press forward with a steadfastness in Christ, having a perfect brightness of hope and a love of God and of all men. Wherefore, if ye shall press forward, feasting upon the word of Christ, and endure to the end, behold, thus saith the Father: Ye shall have eternal life."* - 2 Nephi 31:20	**ANCHOR:** *"It shall come to pass, that the spirits of those who are righteous are received into a state of happiness, which is called paradise, a state of rest, a state of peace, where they shall rest from all their troubles and from all care and sorrow."* - Alma 40:12
LIFESAVER: *"It is as easy to give heed to the word of Christ, which will point to you a straight course to eternal bliss, as it was for our fathers to give heed to this compass, which would point unto them a straight course to the promised land."* - Alma 37:44	**ANCHOR:** *"And thus we can behold how false, and also the unsteadiness of the hearts of the children of men; yea, we can see that the Lord in his great infinite goodness doth bless and prosper those who put their trust in him."* - Helaman 11:1
LIFESAVER: *"Every man receiveth wages of him whom he listeth to obey."* - Alma 3:27	**SUNKEN SHIP:** *"Repent, for the kingdom of heaven is at hand."* - Alma 10:20

Lesson #44	**TIME: I Will Benefit As I Use My Time Wisely** *(Timecard to practice time management)*

YOU'LL NEED: Copy three Timecards (page 97) for each young woman, scissors, and markers.

> *Review Timed scripture search (page 194) and Story and Efficiency Expert's Advice #1-5 (page 196) in Young Women Manual 1*.*

ACTIVITY: Encourage young women to follow the advice of an efficiency expert by using the Timecard to write down the most important tasks to be performed each day for one week. Follow instructions on card.

1. Review the following scriptures on time: Eccles. 3:1, 8:5, D&C 60:13, and 1 Nephi 15:32.
2. Color and cut 7 Timecard forms for the week.
3. Keep a copy of the Timecard to copy later.
4. Follow the Timecard plan and report progress.

COLOR SYMBOL: Color floral symbol on activity and scripture card. File activity in Young Women Value-able Journal behind value tab.

> *Choice & Accountability (orange poppy)*

PERSONAL PROGRESS* GOALS:
Beehive 1 (Choice and Accountability 1)
Beehive 2 (Integrity 2)

THOUGHT TREAT: Self-Esteem Clock Cookies. Frost round sugar cookies with clock numbers 12, 3, 6, and 9. Place licorice in the center for the long and short hands of the clock. Place miniature M&M's where the numbers 1, 2, 4, 5, 7, 8, 10, and 11 should go. Tell young women that if we manage our time each day and do the "must do's" and "should do's" first, then hopefully we will have time for the "would like to dos." Our self-esteem builds when we know we have done our best to do the most important tasks first. Part of the reward for work is the feeling we have when we achieve worthwhile goals. We can easily waste our time by not planning ahead. Without planning we lose sleep, become stressed and unhappy.

MIDWEEK ACTIVITIES:
Time in a Bottle Spin-the-Bottle. Have young women sit in a circle with a bottle in the center full of time hints (see below). Take turns spinning the bottle. The person it points to opens the bottle, takes out a time hint and reads it aloud. Share how this time hint could help you use your time wisely. Place the following hints in bottle. Copy hints for young women to take home.

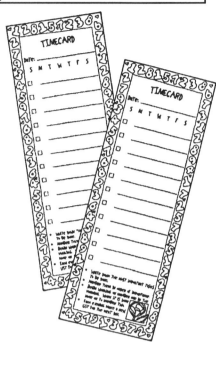

TIME HINTS:
☺ Retire and rise early.
☺ There's a difference between leisure and lazy.
☺ Prioritize tasks to get the most out of your day.
☺ Plan time or others will control your time.
☺ If not 10 minutes early, you're 10 minutes late.
☺ Don't waste your time. Spot time wasters.
☺ Don't let TV rob your time.
☺ Give time to important tasks first when you have energy.
☺ Make a list and check it twice.
☺ Take care of your health, giving you energy to use your time wisely.
☺ Pray daily before planning your time.
☺ Think of your planner as your brain book.
☺ If at first you don't succeed, reschedule.
☺ Goals are only dreams until they are written.
☺ Each day can be the start of a bright future.
☺ Schedule scripture time to lighten your day.
☺ Time is a tool that only you can work.
☺ "Concentration is the secret of strength."

- Ralph Waldo Emerson

TIMECARD

Date: _____

S   M   T   W   T   F   S

☐ _____

☐ _____

☐ _____

☐ _____

☐ _____

☐ _____

☐ _____

☐ _____

☐ _____

☐ _____

☐ _____

- Write down the most important tasks to be done.
- Number them in order of importance.
- Begin working on number one in the morning. When it is done move on to number two.
- Each evening make a new list for the next day.

TIMECARD

Date: _____

S   M   T   W   T   F   S

☐ _____

☐ _____

☐ _____

☐ _____

☐ _____

☐ _____

☐ _____

☐ _____

☐ _____

☐ _____

☐ _____

- Write down the most important tasks to be done.
- Number them in order of importance.
- Begin working on number one in the morning. When it is done move on to number two.
- Each evening make a new list for the next day.

Lesson #45	**WORK:** I Appreciate the Value of Work
	(Attitude Determines Success attitude adjuster journal)

YOU'LL NEED: Copy of attitude adjuster journal (page 99) for each young woman, pencils, and markers.

Review Discussion (page 199) and Teacher presentation (page 201) in Young Women Manual 1*.

ACTIVITY: With this attitude adjuster journal, young women can evaluate what their attitude might be in challenging situations.
1. Write down the results of a negative and a positive attitude in a challenging situation.
2. Talk about work situations and how we struggle to complete tasks. Work can be a drudgery or a joy, depending upon our attitude. For example, a family took care of an elderly grandparent, helping her through each day to overcome the handicaps of old age. They said that when they were negative, it caused stress to the grandparent and stress to the family. When they were positive and patient, it brought joy.

COLOR SYMBOL: Color floral symbols on activity and scripture card. File activity in Young Women Value-able Journal behind value tab.

Good Works (yellow sunflower)

PERSONAL PROGRESS* GOALS:
Beehive 1 (Knowledge 3, Good Works 4, 5, 8)
Beehive 2 (Integrity 2)

THOUGHT TREAT: Fortune Cookies. Give each young woman a fortune cookie and have her read her fortune. Talk about the fortunes and how realistic they are. Talk about creating our own good fortune in life by living the gospel of Jesus Christ. We receive great blessings through obedience. Read D&C 89:18-20. The greatest fortunes are waiting for us—that is, life with Heavenly Father and Jesus. As we work diligently with the right attitude, we can receive great blessings.

My Attitude Determines My Success

Challenge:	Result of a Negative Attitude:	Result of a Positive Attitude:
School Classes		
Baby-sitting		
Developing Talents		
Church Calling		
Home Tasks		
Part-time Job		

Work can be a rewarding experience or drudgery depending on your attitude! With each challenge, write about the results of a negative attitude and a positive attitude. Think about your own situation and what you would change to make it more positive.

MIDWEEK ACTIVITIES:
1. **Find Some Farm Work.** Find a farm and see if young women can do some work on the farm, e.g., feed the birds and animals, milk cows, stack hay, rake, clean, etc.
2. **Unusual Tasks.** Find unique things for young women to do that will benefit the community or them personally. Have all young women help on specific projects, e.g., wash cars, organize with ward members to cater a ward banquet, supply entertainment for ward functions, do dishes after ward activities, put on a play involving children, work with the mentally and physically handicapped, find and adopt a grandparent, entertain at a convalescent center, visit those in nursing homes or rehabilitation centers, organize a patriotic parade, design and put on a play that teaches children or young women values, invite parents to participate in service projects, go on a good will drive to collect items for the needy, cook for a homeless shelter and serve them.

See PERSONAL PROGRESS GOALS (page 64, lesson 30) for other ideas.

My Attitude Determines My Success

Challenge:	Result of a Negative Attitude:	Result of a Positive Attitude:
School Classes		
Baby-sitting		
Developing Talents		
Church Calling		
Home Tasks		
Part-time Job		

Work can be a rewarding experience or drudgery depending on your attitude! With each challenge, write about the results of a negative attitude and a positive attitude. Think about your own situation and what you would change to make it more positive.

Lesson #46	**EDUCATION:** I Will Pursue a Good Education *("Chew"sing a Career! gum wrapped pros and cons)*

YOU'LL NEED: Copy of "Chew"sing a Career! gum holder and career pros and cons gum wrappers (page 101) on lightweight paper for each young woman, pencils, and markers.

> *Review Picture and wordstrip and Quotation and discussion (page 204) in Young Women Manual 1*.*

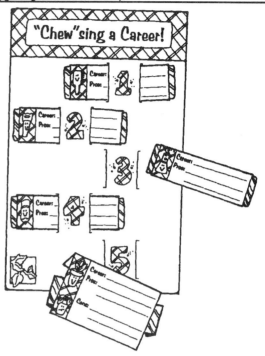

ACTIVITY:

Step #1. Cut out the "Chew"sing a Career" gum holder, cutting a slit on the sides of each number with a razor blade. Place a piece of cardboard underneath when cutting.

Step #2. Color and cut out gum wrappers.

Step #3. Follow instructions on page to write pros and cons on wrappers and slide into a slot indicating career choices.

COLOR SYMBOL: Color floral symbol on activity and scripture card. File activity in Young Women Value-able Journal behind value tab.

> *Knowledge (green ivy)*

PERSONAL PROGRESS* GOALS:

Beehive 1 (Knowledge 1, 7-8)

Beehive 2 (Knowledge 2, 4, 7-8)

Mia Maid 1 (Faith 5-6, Knowledge 9)

Mia Maid 2 (Knowledge 4-6, Choice & Accountability 4)

Laurel 1 & 2 Projects #9-11 (page 79)

THOUGHT TREAT: "Chew"sing a Home Career Gum. Color and cut out "Chew"sing a Career! gum wrappers (page 101) and glue around a stick of gum. Give gum to young women, and discuss possible home careers and the advantages of doing work in the home as they raise their family.

MIDWEEK ACTIVITIES:

1. **Reading Program Assist.** Have young women tutor children in reading. Volunteer at schools or the library.

2. **Teacher Mom Prep.** Tell young women that when they become mothers they will also be teachers. Talk about different areas of education such as math, science, English, history, etc., and why these are so important in raising a family.

3. **"PIG" Seminar.** Tell young women that pigs are very intelligent animals and can teach us a lot. PIGs can also mean "Pretty Intelligent Girls," so invite young women to "hoof on over" with a notebook and pen. Invite four or five of the best professionals you can find to teach a 15-minute seminar on their profession. Have them talk about the ups and downs and pros and cons of their profession. Make pink pig ears for all the girls and tie them on their head with string. Give each girl and speaker a "Pig Hunk" candy bar (BIG HUNK bar with the letter "P" taped over the "B"). Tell young women that the more they learn about various professions, the better chance they will have of getting there. If they wait until their college years to know what they want, they may waste precious time and money. Have a PIG brainstorm before the seminar where young women and leaders can share their "Pretty Intelligent Girl" study habits.

"Chew"sing a Career!

] 1 [

] 2 [

] 3 [

] 4 [

] 5 [

Career: _____
Pros: _____
_____
Cons: _____
_____

Career: _____
Pros: _____
_____
Cons: _____
_____

Career: _____
Pros: _____
_____
Cons: _____
_____

Using each gum wrapper "chew"s the top 5 careers you would like, noting the pros and cons of each. Then slide them into slots indicating your first choice in #1, second choice in #2, etc.

Career: _____
Pros: _____
_____
Cons: _____
_____

Career: _____
Pros: _____
_____
Cons: _____
_____

Lesson #47	**TALENTS:** I Will Develop My Talents *(Hidden Talents crossword puzzle)*

YOU'LL NEED: Copy of crossword puzzle (page 103) for each young woman, pencils, and markers.

> *Review Discussion "Explore some of the ways people discover their talents" (page 207) and Teacher presentation (page 209) in Young Women Manual 1*.*

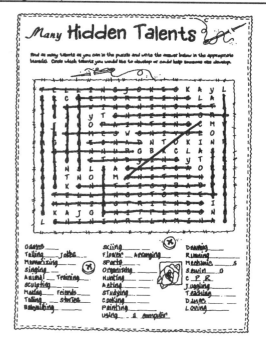

ACTIVITY: Help young women find the many talents they can develop throughout their life. Follow the puzzle instructions to find them. Have young women highlight talents they wish to pursue.

COLOR SYMBOL: Color floral symbol on activity and scripture card. File activity in Young Women Value- able Journal behind value tab.

Individual Worth (red rose)

PERSONAL PROGRESS* GOALS:
<u>Beehive 1</u> (Individual Worth 4, Knowledge 2, 5, Good Works 8)
<u>Beehive 2</u> (Individual Worth 1, 3, 4, 8, Good Works 4, 6)
<u>Mia Maid 1</u> (Individual Worth 2, 4, 5, 8, Knowledge 1-5, Integrity 1)
<u>Mia Maid 2</u> (Knowledge 5, 7, Choice & Accountability 2)
<u>Laurel 1 & 2</u> Project #3 (page 79)

THOUGHT TREAT: <u>Your Favorite Recipe</u>. Share a taste of your favorite recipe and prepare copies of the recipe. Tell young women that to learn to cook they have to invest the time necessary to learn and try various recipes. As with any other talent, the results are worth the effort. Remind them to "Cook up a storm, but don't let the dishes reign." Clean as you go, serving a meal with dishes done.

MIDWEEK ACTIVITIES:
1. <u>Talents, Skits, and Banana Splits</u>. Have an evening with young men and women to share their talents or put on skits. End the evening with banana splits. Have young men and women tell you their talent and how many minutes they will need to perform, then make up the program.(Note: Schedule auditions ahead of time to see how to fit the different talents into the program.)

2. <u>Hidden Talent Night</u>.
<u>Step #1.</u> Research each young woman and have several people she knows tell you of a talent she has. Spotlight each young woman by reading a paragraph about her.
<u>Step #2.</u> Gather pictures of each young woman and display them along with a typewritten spotlight for each.
<u>Step #3.</u> Put a number under each photo displayed on a table. Have young women go around and write something about each young woman on a sheet of cardstock paper in front of picture. You may want to do this before the spotlight.
<u>Step #4.</u> Gather the comments and place them in an envelope with her picture so young women can take these home. They can read and reread the comments and perhaps learn about talents they didn't know they had.

 **Young Women Manual 1* and *Personal Progress* books are published by The Church of Jesus Christ of Latter-day Saints, Salt Lake City, Utah.

Many Hidden Talents

Find as many talents as you can in the puzzle and write the answer below in the appropriate blank(s). Circle which talents you would like to develop or could help someone else develop.

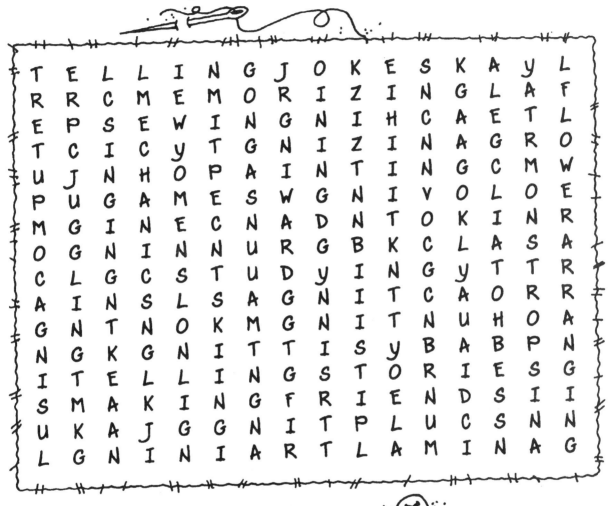

```
T E L L I N G J O K E S K A y L
R R C S M E W M R I Z I N G A L T F
E P C S N Y O I G N I Z I H N C E C L
T U J I G M O M T P E N I N I N A C L O
U G G N A E N E C N N G D I T O G L W
P G I A I S N N S U N I B N V O K I E
M L I C S O U A K G R I K T C K L A R
O I N N S L K A M D G I I N G Y I T A
C N T S O N I M G G y N I O C A A O R
A G K G L L I I G T N I S T B U H R
G T E L I I G N N I I T y R I E A N
N G A K J I G G G I S I S T O N U I S G
I T M N L I G N A F R S T P E L I N
S M K J G I G A I R T P L A M S S I N
U K A N I N G I R T L A M C I S N A
L G N I N I A T L A M C I N A
```

G_____

T_____   J_____

M_____

S_____

A_____   T_____

SC_____

M_____   F_____

T_____   S_____

B_____

SK_____

F_____   A_____

SP_____

O_____

H_____

A_____

ST_____

C_____

P_____

U_____ __ __

D_____

R_____

M_____   S

S_____   G

C_____

J_____

T_____

D_____

L_____

GOALS: I Will Create My Future with Short-range Goals

Lesson #48

(My Future Looks Bright goal planner)

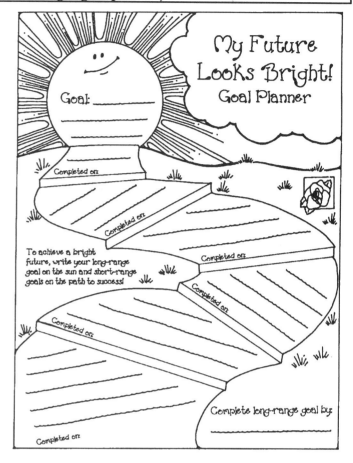

YOU'LL NEED: Copy two planner forms (page 105) for each young woman, pencils, and markers.

Review Introduction Activity (page 212) in Young Women Manual 1*.

ACTIVITY: Help young women realize that their future looks bright as they plan for a sparkling life. With this form they can project what they want to be and what they want to do. Using the form ask young women to "Choose a goal and using the six steps, make short-range goals that help you achieve success!" OPTION: Play the fun licorice game below (see Thought Treat).

COLOR SYMBOL: Color floral symbol on activity and scripture card. File activity in Young Women Value-able Journal behind value tab.

Individual Worth (red rose)

PERSONAL PROGRESS* GOALS:
Beehive 1 (Individual Worth 4, Knowledge 2)
Beehive 2 (Knowledge 5, 6, Integrity 4)
Mia Maid 1 (Integrity 3)
Mia Maid 2 (Divine Nature 6, Individual Worth 2)

THOUGHT TREAT: Long-Range and Short-range Licorice Snacks and GAME. Write on slips of paper 25 long-range goal ideas and 25 short-range goal ideas. Place slips in a container. Have young women take turns drawing goal wordstrips and reading them aloud while the others guess if the goal is long- or short-range. The first three young women to say "short range" or "long range" earn a short or long piece of licorice.

MIDWEEK ACTIVITIES:
1. Play the Brick Wall Game in the Parking Lot.
The objective is to cross the asphalt without touching the ground. Start with five girls and six flat bricks in a line. The sixth brick is placed behind the girls. The girl at the end passes the sixth brick to the person in front and then they all step forward. Have girls continue this until they get from Point A to Point B (and achieve their goal), holding hands to help each other keep their balance. Afterwards, talk about long-range goals, e.g.,

going to the temple, going on a mission, having an eternal family, obtaining an education, spending time quality time with your family now before leaving home.

2. Goal Anticipation Exercises. Have young women think of ways they can anticipate their future, looking forward to the next goal.

Step #1. They can make an "anticipation poster" with a long-range goal and begin collecting pictures that remind them of their goal (e.g., for a trip to Hawaii, they can collect brochures, find pictures of tropical treats and a girl in a bathing suit, even place sand in a bag and attach to poster to anticipate the sand on the beach. Have them write their goal on the poster, when they plan to go, and the steps needed to achieve their goal.

Step #2. Give each young woman a "goal/project" notebook she can use to list long-range goals and projects (one on each page). Encourage young women to fill the book, then make a numerical or A-Z contents or index to cross-reference the goal or project.

My Future Looks Bright!
Goal Planner

Goal: _____

_____

_____

Completed on:

Completed on:

Completed on:

Completed on:

To achieve a bright future, write your long-range goal on the sun and short-range goals on the path to success!

Completed on:

Completed on:

Complete long-range goal by:

_____

Lesson #49	**LEADERSHIP:** I Will Delegate and Show Encouragement
	(Be a Delegator Alligator! assignment planner)

YOU'LL NEED: Two copies of the Alligator! assignment planner (page 107) for each young woman, pencils, and markers.

Review Role play and Lesson Application (pages 216-217) in Young Women Manual 1*.

ACTIVITY: Help young women learn how to delegate assignments when they are in leadership positions. Use the first copy of the Assignment Delegation Plan to role-play receiving an assignment and planning it. Ask them to use the second copy as their master original to copy and place in their notebooks. Encourage them to use this form whenever they are in a leadership position in their family, at church, school, or in the community.

COLOR SYMBOL: Color floral symbol on activity and scripture card. File activity in Young Women Value-able Journal behind value tab.

Individual Worth (red rose)

PERSONAL PROGRESS* GOALS:
Beehive 1 (Knowledge 3)
Beehive 2 (Knowledge 4, Integrity 2)
Mia Maid 1 (Individual Worth 4, Knowledge 5, Good Works 8)
Laurel 1 & 2 Project #2 (page 79)

THOUGHT TREAT: Thank-You Treats.
Encourage young women to make thank-you notes extra special by attaching them to objects or using stickers.
NOTE IDEAS: "Your work is so appealing" (attach note to a banana), "You're a Big Hunk for helping" (attach note to Big Hunk candy when thanking a young man), "You did a 'soup-er' job" (attach note to a can of soup), "You were 'mint' to help on our project. Thanks!" (Attach starlight mint or peppermint patty to note). Encourage young women to share ideas.

MIDWEEK ACTIVITIES:
1. Picnic and Volleyball. Plan a picnic with the young women. Let them make plans and delegate assignments. (Option: Have some "forget" their assignment, e.g., forget the napkins; forget utensils and bring only the knife, so young women must eat with knives; forget the dessert, but have one ready to serve after volleyball). Observe how the picnic works out, then discuss what happens when people don't follow through on their assignments. Plan volleyball and pretend to forget the ball. Really ham it up and have fun.

2. Balloon Volleyball. To make a net, tie a string from one end of the room to the other at eye level. Blow up two large balloons of two different colors, one for each team.
Step #1. **Leader vs. Young Women Competition.** Have leaders and young women compete in balloon volleyball. Have young women and leaders mixed on both sides of the net. Leaders play with one balloon, e.g., yellow, hitting the balloon to the other leaders. Young women play with another balloon, e.g., blue, hitting the blue balloon to the other young women. The leaders can't hit the young women's blue balloon and the young women can't hit the leaders' yellow balloon. Both teams serve their balloon at the same time from any place behind the net. Leaders can invite parents to help create an even team. Switch colors after a while.
Step #2. **Team Work Competition.** Discuss what it means when responsibilities are delegated among team members. Talk about team work and expectations. Talk about consideration when team members don't play well. Play again using one balloon with leaders and girls in each team.

Be a

Delegator Alligator!

Share responsibilities with others in the pond.

- Assignment: _____

  _____

- Importance of the assignment: _____

  _____

- Who will do what and when? _____

  _____

  _____

  _____

  _____

  _____

- When to follow up on the assignment: _____

  _____

- Don't forget to express encouragement and thanks!

Front cover

My Testimony Grows as I Study the Scriptures

Name: _____

Back cover

My Testimony Grows as I Study the Scriptures

I love ♡ to read the scriptures because they help my testimony to blossom and grow. Blessings come from reading the scriptures and obeying the commandments. "Thou shalt be like a watered garden" (Isaiah 58:2-14). With the scriptures I can "BLOOM WHERE I'M PLANTED." Each week in Young Women I will receive a scripture that represents the value taught in the lesson. Then I will:

1. Find the scripture and fill in the missing words.
2. Color the value symbol the value color written at the bottom of the card. Example: Color the poppy (shown right) "orange," representing the value "Choice and Accountability."
3. Post scripture cards on my mirror during the week to ponder (Moroni 10:4-5).
4. OPTION #1: Create a book by punching the two hearts (shown left) and tie a ribbon through holes in a bow.

OPTION #2: Cut the heart border off and create a card file with A-Z dividers (to file cards by subject), or Young Women value divider tabs.

Inside first page

My Testimony Grows as I Study the Scriptures

HEAVENLY FATHER: I am a Daughter of God

D&C 88:63 "Draw near unto me and I will draw near unto you; __ __ __ __ me diligently and ye shall __ __ __ __ me; __ __ __, and ye shall receive; __ __ __ __ __, and it shall be opened unto you."

Young Women Value: Divine Nature (blue morning glory) Lesson #1 Manual 1

My Testimony Grows as I Study the Scriptures

JESUS CHRIST: I Will Think of My Savior

Alma 11:40 "And he shall come into the
__ __ __ __ __ __ to __ __ __ __ __ __ his people;
and he shall take upon him the transgressions
of those who __ __ __ __ __ __ __ __ on his
name; and these are they that cometh to
none else."

Young Women Value: Faith (white lily) Lesson #2 Manual 1

My Testimony Grows as I Study the Scriptures

EXAMPLE: I Will Follow the Example of Jesus

2 Nephi 31:9-10 "[Jesus' baptism] showeth unto the children
of men the straitness of the __ __ __ __, and the narrowness
of the __ __ __ __, by which they should
__ __ __ __ __, he having set the example before
them. And he said unto the children of men:
__ __ __ __ __ __ thou me. Wherefore, my beloved
brethren, can we follow Jesus save we shall be
willing to keep the commandments of the Father?"

Young Women Value: Divine Nature (blue morning glory) Lesson #3 Manual 1

My Testimony Grows as I Study the Scriptures

HOLY GHOST: I Will Seek the Companionship of the Holy Ghost

Moroni 10-4-5 "And when ye shall receive
these things, I would exhort you that ye would
ask God, the Eternal Father, in the name of
Christ, if these things are not __ __ __ __; and
if ye shall ask with a sincere __ __ __ __ __
with real intent, having faith in Christ, he will
manifest the truth of it unto you. And by the power of the Holy
Ghost ye may know the __ __ __ __ __ of all things."

Young Women Value: Divine Nature (blue morning glory) Lesson #4 Manual 1

| My Testimony Grows as I Study the Scriptures |

POTENTIAL: I Will Seek to Develop My Divine Potential

Moroni 10:32 "Yea, come unto Christ, and be perfected in him, and __ __ __ __ yourself of all ungodliness; and if ye shall deny yourself of all ungodliness, and love God with all your __ __ __ __ __, __ __ __ __ and strength, then is his grace sufficient for you, that by his grace ye shall be perfect in Christ; and if by the grace of God ye are perfect in Christ, ye can nowise __ __ __ __ the power of God."

Young Women Value: Divine Nature (blue morning glory) Lesson #5 Manual 1

| My Testimony Grows as I Study the Scriptures |

HAPPINESS: I Will Find Joy in Everyday Living

Alma 41:10 "Do not suppose, because it has been spoken concerning restoration, that ye shall be __ __ __ __ __ __ __ __ from __ __ __ to happiness, Behold, I say unto you, wickedness never was happiness."

John 13:17 "If ye know these things, happy are ye if ye __ __ them."

Young Women Value: Choice & Accountability (orange poppy) Lesson #6 Manual 1

| My Testimony Grows as I Study the Scriptures |

HOMEMAKING: I Will Find Joy in Homemaking

D&C 109:8 "Organize yourselves; __ __ __ __ __ __ __ every needful thing, and establish a __ __ __ __ __ __ , even a house of prayer, a house of fasting, a house of faith, a house of learning, a house of glory, a house of __ __ __ __ __ __ , a house of God; That your incomings may be in the name of the Lord, that your outgoings may be in the name of the Lord."

Young Women Value: Good Works (yellow sunflower) Lesson #7 Manual 1

| My Testimony Grows as I Study the Scriptures |

ATTITUDE: I Want to Be the Best Possible Wife and Mother

D&C 25:14-15 "Continue in the spirit of meekness, and beware of __ __ __ __ __ __. Let thy soul __ __ __ __ __ __ __ __ in thy husband, and the glory which shall come upon him. Keep my commandments continually, and a __ __ __ __ __ __ of righteousness thou shalt receive. And except thou do this, where I am you __ __ __ __ __ __ __ come."

Young Women Value: Individual Worth (red rose) Lesson #8 Manual 1

| My Testimony Grows as I Study the Scriptures |

HONORING PARENTS: I Will Improve My Relationships

Colossians 3:20 "Children, __ __ __ __ __ your parents in __ __ [righteous] things: for this is well pleasing unto the Lord."

Mosiah 13:20 "Honor thy father and thy mother, that thy __ __ __ __ may be __ __ __ __ upon the land which the Lord thy God giveth thee."

Young Women Value: Individual Worth (red rose) Lesson #9 Manual 1

| My Testimony Grows as I Study the Scriptures |

FAMILY SUPPORT: I Will Support and Be Loyal to My Family

D&C 108:7 "Therefore, __ __ __ __ __ __ __ __ __ __ __ your brethren in all your conversation, in all your __ __ __ __ __ __ __, in all your exhortations, and in all your __ __ __ __ __ __."

Young Women Value: Individual Worth (red rose) Lesson #10 Manual 1

My Testimony Grows as I Study the Scriptures

SELF-RELIANCE: I Will Follow My Savior

D&C 58:27-28 "Verily I say, men should be anxiously engaged in a good _ _ _ _ _, and do many things of their own _ _ _ _ will, and bring to pass much

_ _ _ _ _ _ _ _ _ _ _ _ _ _ _ _;
For the power is in them, wherein they are

_ _ _ _ _ _ _ unto themselves. And inasmuch as men do _ _ _ _ _ they shall in nowise lose their _ _ _ _ _ _ _."

Young Women Value: Divine Nature (blue morning glory) Lesson #11 Manual 1

My Testimony Grows as I Study the Scriptures

SELF-RELIANCE: I Will Strengthen Family Relationships

Ephesians 6:1-4 "Children, _ _ _ _ _ your parents in the _ _ _ _: for this is right. _ _ _ _ _ _ thy father and mother; (which is the first commandment with

_ _ _ _ _ _ _;) That it may be well with thee, and thou mayest _ _ _ _ long on the earth. And, ye fathers, provoke not your children to _ _ _ _ _: but bring them up in the nurture and admonition of the Lord."

Young Women Value: Individual Worth (red rose) Lesson #12 Manual 1

My Testimony Grows as I Study the Scriptures

PRIESTHOOD: I Honor Priesthood Bearers

D&C 121:45 "Let thy bowels also be full of _ _ _ _ _ _ _ _ towards all men, and to the household of faith, and let

_ _ _ _ _ _ _ garnish thy thoughts unceasingly; then shall thy confidence wax

_ _ _ _ _ _ _ in the presence of God; and the doctrine of the priesthood shall distil upon thy _ _ _ _ _ as the dews from heaven."

Young Women Value: Individual Worth (red rose) Lesson #13 Manual 1

My Testimony Grows as I Study the Scriptures

SELF-RELIANCE: I Will Support My Father in Righteousness

D&C 121:36 "The rights of the priesthood are inseparably connected with the powers of __ __ __ __ __ __, and ... the powers of heaven cannot be controlled nor handled only upon the principles of __ __ __ __ __ __ __ __ __ __ __ __ __."

Young Women Value: Individual Worth (red rose) Lesson #14 Manual 1

My Testimony Grows as I Study the Scriptures

PRIESTHOOD: Understanding Melchizedek Priesthood Responsibilities

D&C 84: 19-22 "This __ __ __ __ __ __ __ priesthood administereth the gospel and holdeth the __ __ __ of the mysteries of the kingdom, even the key of the knowledge of __ __ __. Therefore, in the ordinances thereof, the power of godliness is manifest. And without the ordinances thereof, and the authority of that priesthood, the __ __ __ __ __ of godliness is not manifest unto men in the flesh; For without this no man can see the face of God, even the Father, and live."

Young Women Value: Individual Worth (red rose) Lesson #15 Manual 1

My Testimony Grows as I Study the Scriptures

PRIESTHOOD: I Will Support My Celestial Companion

Genesis 2:18, 24 "And the Lord God said, It is not __ __ __ __ that the man should be __ __ __ __ __; I will make him an __ __ __ __ meet for him. Therefore shall a man leave his father and his mother, and shall __ __ __ __ __ __ unto his wife: and they shall be one flesh."

Young Women Value: Individual Worth (red rose) Lesson #16 Manual 1

♡

♡

My Testimony Grows as I Study the Scriptures

COVENANTS & ORDINANCES: I Will Keep Sacred Promises

D&C 82:9-10 "I give unto you directions how you may _ _ _ before me, that it may turn to you for your _ _ _ _ _ _ _ _ _ _ _. I, the Lord, am _ _ _ _ _ _ when ye do what I say; but when ye do _ _ _ what I say, ye have no _ _ _ _ _ _ _."

Young Women Value: Divine Nature (blue morning glory) Lesson #17 Manual 1

♡

♡

My Testimony Grows as I Study the Scriptures

FAMILIES FOREVER: Temple Marriage Brings Eternal Family Life

D&C 132:19 "If a man _ _ _ _ _ _ a wife by my word, which is my _ _ _ _, and by the new and everlasting covenant, and it is sealed unto them by the Holy Spirit of _ _ _ _ _ _ _ _, by him who is anointed, unto whom I have appointed this power and the keys of this priesthood ... [ye] shall inherit thrones, kingdoms, principalities, and powers, dominions ... and if ye _ _ _ _ _ _ in my covenant ... [there] shall be a fulness and continuation of the _ _ _ _ _ forever and ever."

Young Women Value: Individual Worth (red rose) Lesson #18 Manual 1

♡

♡

My Testimony Grows as I Study the Scriptures

RECORDS: I Will Make Personal Records of My Life

2 Nephi 25:23 "For we labor diligently to _ _ _ _ _ _, to persuade our children, and also our brethren, to _ _ _ _ _ _ _ _ in Christ, and to be reconciled to God; for we know that it is by grace that we are saved, after _ _ _ we can do."

Young Women Value: Individual Worth (red rose) Lesson #19 Manual 1

My Testimony Grows as I Study the Scriptures

FRIENDSHIP: I Will Extend My Friendship

Matthew 5:15-16 "Neither do men __ __ __ __ __ a candle, and put it under a bushel, but on a candlestick; and it giveth light unto all that are in the house. Let your light so __ __ __ __ __ before men, that they may see your __ __ __ __ works, and glorify your Father which is in heaven."

Young Women Value: Good Works (yellow sunflower)   Lesson #20 Manual 1

My Testimony Grows as I Study the Scriptures

EXAMPLE: I Will Set a Righteous Example

1 Timothy 4:12 "Let no man despise thy youth; but be thou an example of the believers in __ __ __ __, in conversation, in charity, in spirit, in faith, in __ __ __ __ __ __."

Young Women Value: Choice and Accountability (orange poppy) Lesson #21 Manual 1

My Testimony Grows as I Study the Scriptures

REPENTANCE: I Will Understand the Principle of Repentance

Mosiah 27:29 "My __ __ __ __ hath been redeemed from the gall of bitterness and bonds of iniquity. I was in the darkness abyss; but now I behold the marvelous __ __ __ __ __ of God. My soul was racked with eternal torment; but I am snatched [saved from danger], and my soul is __ __ __ __ __ __ no more."

Young Women Value: Choice and Accountability (orange poppy) Lesson #22 Manual 1

My Testimony Grows as I Study the Scriptures

FORGIVENESS: I Will Forgive Others

Matthew 5:43 "Ye have heard that it hath been said, Thou shalt __ __ __ __ thy neighbour, and hate thine enemy. But I say unto you, __ __ __ __ your enemies, __ __ __ __ __ them that curse you, do __ __ __ __ to them that hate you, and __ __ __ __ for them which despitefully use you, and persecute you."

Young Women Value: Individual Worth (red rose) Lesson #23 Manual 1

My Testimony Grows as I Study the Scriptures

PRAYER & MEDITATION: I Value Daily Prayer and Mediation

Alma 34:27 "Yea, and when you do not cry unto the Lord, let your hearts be __ __ __ __, drawn out in prayer unto him continually for your __ __ __ __ __ __ __, and also for the welfare of those who are around you."

Young Women Value: Faith (white lily) Lesson #24 Manual 1

My Testimony Grows as I Study the Scriptures

SABBATH: I Will Choose Worthy Sabbath Day Activities

D&C 59:8-10 "Thou shalt offer a sacrifice unto the Lord thy God in righteousness, even that of a broken heart and a contrite __ __ __ __ __ __ __. And that thou mayest more fully keep thyself unspotted from the world, thou shalt go to the __ __ __ __ __ of prayer and offer up thy sacraments upon my holy day; For verily this is a day appointed unto you to __ __ __ __ from your labors, and to pay thy devotions unto the Most High."

Young Women Value: Choice and Accountability (orange poppy) Lesson #25 Manual 1

My Testimony Grows as I Study the Scriptures

TESTIMONY: I Will Strengthen and Share My Testimony

Alma 32:28-29 "Compare the __ __ __ __ unto a seed ... planted in your __ __ __ __ __ ... if ye do not cast it out by your unbelief ... it will begin to swell within your breasts; and when you feel these swelling motions, ye will begin to say within yourselves—It must needs be that this is a good seed, or that the word is good, for it beginneth to enlarge my __ __ __ __; yea, it beginneth to enlighten my understanding, yea, it beginneth to be delicious to me."

Young Women Value: Individual Worth (red rose) Lesson #26 Manual 1

My Testimony Grows as I Study the Scriptures

SCRIPTURES: I Will Study the Scriptures Daily

2 Nephi 33:4-5 "I know that the Lord God will consecrate my prayers for the gain of my people. And the words which I have written in weakness will be made strong unto them; for it persuadeth them to do __ __ __ __; it maketh known unto them of their fathers; and it speaketh of Jesus and persuadeth them to __ __ __ __ __ __ __ in him, and to endure to the end, which is life eternal."

Young Women Value: Knowledge (green ivy) Lesson #27 Manual 1

My Testimony Grows as I Study the Scriptures

TEMPTATION: I Must Be Strong to Resist Temptation

2 Nephi 2:27-28 "Men are free according to the flesh; and all things are given them which are expedient unto man. And they are free to __ __ __ __ __ __ liberty and eternal life, through the great Mediator of all men, or to choose __ __ __ __ __ __ __ __ __ and death, according to the captivity and power of the devil; for he seeketh that all men might be miserable like unto himself. And now, my sons, I would that ye should look to the great Mediator, and hearken unto his great commandments; and be faithful unto his words, and choose eternal life according to the will of his Holy Spirit."

Young Women Value: Choice & Accountability (orange poppy) Lesson #28 Manual 1

My Testimony Grows as I Study the Scriptures

SECOND COMING: I Will Prepare for the Coming of Jesus

Moroni 7:48 "Pray unto the Father with all the energy of heart, that ye may be filled with this love, which he hath bestowed upon all who are true followers of his Son, Jesus Christ; that ye may __ __ __ __ __ __ the sons of God; that when he shall __ __ __ __ __ __ we shall __ __ like him, for we shall see him as he is; that we may have this hope; that we may be purified even as he is __ __ __ __. Amen."

Young Women Value: Integrity (purple pansy) Lesson #29 Manual 1

My Testimony Grows as I Study the Scriptures

SERVICE: I Will Find Joy in Service

D&C 81:5-6 "Wherefore, be faithful; stand in the office which I have appointed unto you; succor the __ __ __ __, lift up the hands which hang down, and strengthen the feeble knees. And if thou art faithful unto the end thou shalt have a __ __ __ __ __ of immortality, and eternal life in the mansions which I have prepared in the house of my Father."

Young Women Value: Good Works (yellow sunflower) Lesson #30 Manual 1

My Testimony Grows as I Study the Scriptures

DATING: I Will Seek Wholesome Group Activities

D&C 6:32-33 "Where __ __ __ or __ __ __ __ __ are gathered together in my name ... there will I be in the midst of them—even so am I in the midst of them. Fear not to do good, my sons, for whatsoever ye sow, that shall ye also reap; therefore, if ye sow good ye shall also reap __ __ __ __ for your __ __ __ __ __ __."

Young Women Value: Choice and Accountability (orange poppy) Lesson #31 Manual 1

♡

♡

| My Testimony Grows as I Study the Scriptures |

PURITY: Self-discipline Helps Me Live a Virtuous Life

D&C 56:18 "Blessed are the poor who are

_ _ _ _ _ in heart, whose hearts are

_ _ _ _ _ _ _ _, and whose spirits are contrite,

for they shall see the kingdom of God coming in

power and great glory unto their deliverance; for

the fatness of the earth shall be theirs."

Young Women Value: Choice and Accountability (orange poppy) Lesson #32 Manual 1

♡

♡

| My Testimony Grows as I Study the Scriptures |

MEDIA INFLUENCES: I Will Avoid Degrading Media

Alma 18:32 "He looketh down upon all

the children of men; and he knows all the

_ _ _ _ _ _ _ _ _ and intents of the heart;

for by his hand were they all created from the beginning."

Young Women Value: Choice and Accountability (orange poppy) Lesson #33 Manual 1

♡

♡

| My Testimony Grows as I Study the Scriptures |

VIRTUE: My Virtuous Thoughts Lead to a Virtuous Life

D&C 121:45 "Let virtue garnish thy

thoughts unceasingly; then shall thy

confidence wax _ _ _ _ _ _ in the

presence of God."

Young Women Value: Choice and Accountability (orange poppy) Lesson #34 Manual 1

My Testimony Grows as I Study the Scriptures

RIGHTEOUSNESS: I Can Live Righteously

Proverbs 29:18 "Where there is no vision, the people perish: but he that keepeth the __ __ __, happy is he."

D&C 14:7 "If you __ __ __ __ my commandments and __ __ __ __ __ __ to the end you shall have eternal life, which __ __ __ __ is the greatest of all the gifts of God."

Young Women Value: Integrity (purple pansy) Lesson #35 Manual 1

My Testimony Grows as I Study the Scriptures

VIRTUE AND TRUTH: I Seek Truth and a Virtuous Life

D&C 1:39 "The Lord is God, and the __ __ __ __ __ __ beareth record, and the record is __ __ __ __, and the truth abideth forever and ever."

D&C 93:28 "He that keepeth his commandments receiveth __ __ __ __ __ and light, until he is glorified in truth and knoweth all things."

Young Women Value: Choice and Accountability (orange poppy) Lesson #36 Manual 1

My Testimony Grows as I Study the Scriptures

SELF-CARE: I Will Keep My Body and Mind in Condition

D&C 88:124 "Cease to be __ __ __ __; cease to be unclean; cease to find fault one with another; cease to __ __ __ __ __ longer than is needful; retire to thy bed early, that ye may not be __ __ __ __ __; arise early, that your bodies and your minds may be invigorated."

Young Women Value: Individual Worth (red rose) Lesson #37 Manual 1

My Testimony Grows as I Study the Scriptures

WORD OF WISDOM: I Will Practice Good Nutrition

D&C 89:18-21 "All saints who remember to keep and do these sayings, walking in obedience to the commandments, shall receive __ __ __ __ __ __ in their navel and marrow to their bones; And shall find wisdom and great treasures of knowledge, even __ __ __ __ __ __ treasures; And shall __ __ __ and not be weary, and shall walk and not faint. And I, the Lord, give unto them a promise, that the destroying angel shall __ __ __ __ by them, as the children of Israel, and not __ __ __ __ them. Amen."

Young Women Value: Individual Worth (red rose) Lesson #38 Manual 1

My Testimony Grows as I Study the Scriptures

DRUG ABUSE Affects My Body and Spirit

1 Corinthians 3:16-17 "Know ye not that ye are the __ __ __ __ __ __ of God, and that the Spirit of God dwelleth in __ __ __? If any man defile the temple of God, him shall God destroy; for the temple of God is __ __ __ __, which temple ye are."

Young Women Value: Individual Worth (red rose) Lesson #39 Manual 1

My Testimony Grows as I Study the Scriptures
HEALTH CARE:
I Will Prepare and Provide Basic Health Care Skills in My Home

D&C 38:30 "I tell you these things because of your __ __ __ __ __ __ __ __; wherefore, treasure up __ __ __ __ __ __ __ in your bosoms, lest the wickedness of men revile these things unto you by their wickedness, in a manner which shall speak in your ears with a voice louder than which shall shake the earth; but if ye are __ __ __ __ __ __ __ __ ye shall not __ __ __ __."

Young Women Value: Knowledge (green ivy) Lesson #40 Manual 1

My Testimony Grows as I Study the Scriptures

SUCCESS: I Recognize My Ability to Succeed

Joshua 1:8-9 "This book of the law shall not depart out of thy mouth; but thou shalt meditate therein day and night, that thou mayest __ __ __ __ __ __ __ to do according to all that is written therein: for then thou shalt make thy way prosperous, and then thou shalt have __ __ __ __ success. Have I not commanded thee? Be __ __ __ __ __ __ and of a good courage; be not afraid, neither be thou dismayed: for the Lord thy God is with thee whithersoever thou goest."

Young Women Value: Choice and Accountability (orange poppy) Lesson #41 Manual 1

My Testimony Grows as I Study the Scriptures

SELF-IMPROVEMENT: I Will Accept Opportunities to Improve

D&C 109:14-15 "All those who shall worship in this house may be taught words of wisdom out of the best books, and that they may seek learning even by __ __ __ __ __, and also by __ __ __ __ __, as thou hast said; And that they may grow up in thee, and receive a __ __ __ __ __ __ __ __ of the Holy Ghost, and be organized according to thy laws, and be prepared to obtain every __ __ __ __ __ __ __ thing."

Young Women Value: Individual Worth (red rose) Lesson #42 Manual 1

My Testimony Grows as I Study the Scriptures

RIGHTEOUSNESS: Self-esteem Comes from Righteous Living

Isaiah 58:10-11 "And if thou draw out thy soul to the hungry, and satisfy the afflicted soul; then shall thy __ __ __ __ __ __ rise in obscurity, and thy darkness be as the noonday. And the Lord shall guide thee continually, and satisfy thy soul in drought, and make __ __ __ thy bones: and thou shalt be like a watered garden, and like a spring of water, whose waters __ __ __ __ not."

Young Women Value: Integrity (purple pansy) Lesson #43 Manual 1

My Testimony Grows as I Study the Scriptures

TIME: I Will Benefit As I Use My Time Wisely

Ecclesiastes 3:1 "To every thing there is a
_ _ _ _ _ _ _, and a time to every
_ _ _ _ _ _ _ _ under the heaven."

D&C 60:13 "Thou shalt not _ _ _ _ away thy time, neither
shalt thou bury thy _ _ _ _ _ _ that it may not be
known."

Young Women Value: Choice and Accountability (orange poppy) Lesson #44 Manual 1

My Testimony Grows as I Study the Scriptures

WORK: I Appreciate the Value of Work

D&C 58:26-28 "It is not meet that I should command
you in all things; for he that is compelled in all things
the same is a _ _ _ _ _ _ _ _ and not a wise
servant; wherefore he receiveth no reward. Verily I say,
men should be anxiously engaged in a good _ _ _ _ _,
and do many things of their own free will, and bring to pass much
righteousness. For the power is in them, wherein they are
_ _ _ _ _ _ unto themselves. And inasmuch as men do good
they shall in nowise lose their reward."

Young Women Value: Good Works (yellow sunflower) Lesson #45 Manual 1

My Testimony Grows as I Study the Scriptures

EDUCATION: I Will Pursue a Good Education

D&C 88:77-80 "Teach ye diligently and my grace shall
attend you, that you may be instructed more perfectly in
theory, in principle, in doctrine, in the law of the gospel, in
all _ _ _ _ _ _ that pertain unto the kingdom of
_ _ _ _, that are expedient for you to understand. Of things both in
heaven and in the _ _ _ _ _ _, and under the earth; things which
have been, things which are, things which must shortly come to pass;
things which are at home, things which are abroad ... that ye may be
prepared."

Young Women Value: Knowledge (green ivy) Lesson #46 Manual 1

My Testimony Grows as I Study the Scriptures

TALENTS: I Will Develop My Talents

Moroni 10:18, 30 "And I would exhort you,
my beloved brethren, that ye remember that every
__ __ __ __ gift cometh of Christ. I would exhort you that ye
would __ __ __ __ unto Christ, and lay hold upon every good
__ __ __ __ __, and touch not the evil gift, nor the unclean thing."

Young Women Value: Individual Worth (red rose) Lesson #47 Manual 1

My Testimony Grows as I Study the Scriptures

GOALS: I Will Create My Future with Short-range Goals

1 Nephi 9:6 "The Lord knoweth all things from the
beginning; wherefore, he __ __ __ __ __ __ __ __ __ __
a way to accomplish all his __ __ __ __ __ among
the children of men; for behold, he hath all power unto the
fulfilling of all his words."

Young Women Value: Individual Worth (red rose) Lesson #48 Manual 1

My Testimony Grows as I Study the Scriptures

LEADERSHIP: I Will Delegate and Show Encouragement

D&C 107:99-100 "Let every man learn his
__ __ __ __ __, and to act in the office in which he is
appointed, in all diligence. He that is
__ __ __ __ __ __ __ __ shall not be counted worthy to stand,
and he that learns __ __ __ his duty and shows himself not
approved shall not be counted worthy to __ __ __ __ __."

Young Women Value: Individual Worth (red rose) Lesson #49 Manual 1